CI

5 Books in 1: C   ;;
Cricut Maker; Cricut Design Space;
Cricut Project Ideas; Make Money
with Cricut; The Complete Guide to
Master Your Cricut Maker, Explore
Air 2 and Joy

CRICUT FOR BEGINNERS

The Ultimate Step-by-Step Guide to Get the Ball Rolling with Cricut

Introduction

Cricut machine will help you cut any material you want and create beautiful patterns using the accompanying design software. This software design tool can come with a preloaded design ready to go right out of the box. You can make your unique designs, use an existing design, and update the designs as well. The containers are also filled with many designs to choose from.

You can buy these machines from an online store or a craft store. And the price will depend on the model you choose. The price can also range from $ 100 to $ 350 (and up), so it's best to limit your needs and go for it. Anything that makes your job more comfortable and efficient can be considered a significant investment. Cricut is one of them. It is nice and fun to use. Everyone can benefit from this. We have Cricut in places we never imagined it would be in years past because of its effectiveness.

We have Cricut in offices and workshops. Sound weird to you? This should not be the case because Cricut is never intended to be a homemade tool. It saves time and makes your work so professional, and the good thing is that there are no limits; you can do everything you can. If you are reading this book, you have a Cricut machine at your disposal, and you may not know how to use it. Well, I'm here to help you with that.

The Cricut machine has a pedigree. Yes, the Cricut you have now was not like this a few years ago. But we should not worry about the past and the future and a little about the present. First, we have the manufacturer Cricut, which is a used machine with drawing space. This Cricut maker has cloud-based web software. And this specific series or design cannot work on its own, you have to use the design space on a desktop or laptop, and of course, an internet connection is required.

Another special feature provided by the maker of Cricut is that you can use the offline feature in the spatial design app as long as you use the design app on an iOS device, i.e., iPad / iPhone or MacBook. This means that you can make plans and everything offline. It is just one device, and it's not just because each device has its quirks that add to the general feature that we all know about.

This product has generated so much sales revenue in such a short time due to its effectiveness and practicality. Cricut machine has been in work for years, and it blows everyone's mind and any other cutting machine out there. They keep bringing more and more to the table, and they keep adding something new now and then. The Cricut has dominated that market because of its durability, firmware, performance, and reliability. Some designs are portable and convenient to carry. So, let's go more in-depth in the word of Cricut, and if you like this book, please leave a review after finishing it!

Cricut Basics: What Is Cricut and Why Do You Need It?

If you picked up this book, you most likely know that a Cricut machine can help make all sorts of useful shapes for your artwork or hobby. But what exactly does this machine do and how does it work?

If you decided to purchase one of these neat tools, you were probably drawn by the possibility of streamlining the cutting of different shapes on various materials. You might imagine using Cricut to easily make a piece of clothing, a decoration, fun refrigerator magnets, stickers, or even an ornamental mini-shelf for your living room. Perhaps you're wondering if all these things are possible to do with Cricut, and if so, what type of machine will you need and how much will the work cost. Keep reading to find out the answers to these questions (and so much more!).

What Is a Cricut Machine?

A Cricut is a device that can help you streamline your cutting of different types of materials. This is useful if you don't have enough time, skill, or precision to do your manual cutting. You can use it to make ornaments, shirts, or all kinds of useful stickers with laser precision and accuracy (Sund, 2010).

Cricut is a brand that features multiple products. They carry embossers and heat presses, but more importantly, they feature die-cutting machines that ended up becoming a household name. A Cricut machine is a die-cutting apparatus that you can use at home for your creative projects, artwork, and crafts. However, there is a twist with these machines that makes them unique and highly convenient. They are smart machines that can cut all sorts of shapes out of paper, vinyl, thin plates of cardboard, all sorts of MDF (medium-density fiberboard), wood, and other materials.

Moreover, the latest versions of Cricut machines can also draw with pens. They can score your paper or cardboard for easy and precise folding (think next-level—intricate yet effortless origami artwork, for example).

The Cricut name alone refers to the brand, but their die-cutting machines' popularity made its use synonymous with these specific cutters. While the limits to the utilization of Cricut cutters solely depend on your imagination, the mechanics behind how they operate are a different issue. The proper use of Cricut machines requires understanding how they work and how they should be used to get the best value for your investment.

How Do Cricut Die-Cutting Machines Work?

Cricut machine cutters operate simply and conveniently. First, you need to create a design, which needs to be in an image form, on your computer. After this, you need to send your shape to the cutting machine via a Bluetooth connection or a USB cable.

After the machine receives the right shape to be cut, it then operates its computer, navigating a cutting blade. The principle is similar to how a printer works with its ink nozzle, but here, the machine's computer guides the plate to cut an exact copy of the shape that you created on your computer.

Aside from cutting, the newest Cricut models can emboss, engrave, score, and write using the same principle. This means that working with a Cricut machine covers three main operations:

- Creating your design
- Sending it to the machine and telling it what to do (cut, write, engrave, etc.)
- Doing the hard work while you sit back and sip on your coffee.

Your Cricut machine will come with a couple of add-ons, like different cutter models, cords, instructions, a cutting mat, and more. You will also receive a USB cable and a power adapter, and even one or two dozen projects that you can start making as soon as you plug in your machine. Depending on the model you choose, you can get a special writing pen and scoring wheels.

As you can see, the Cricut die-cutting machine isn't a simple cutter. For example, let's say you want to make your wedding invitations. A Cricut lets you design the layout and text, size, and shape right on your computer. After that, all you need to do is get the correct type of paper ready, insert it into the machine, and let it cut out the card shapes, draw on the text, and score your wedding invitations for folding if needed. Neat, right?

No longer will you need to make an order, then wait to see if your invitations turned out well nor will you have to send the cards back if the writing is wrong. The machine also results in much lower expenses, and arguably, much more convenience since you are creating just the type of card you envisioned.

The trick with using Cricut machines is that you'll have to learn how to work with each model's specific brand software, free to download. This book will help you do that as well, so relax and enjoy the read!

Aside from the brand's software, you can also use other apps compatible with the machine, but this book will focus on creating designs and images from scratch on the brand's app.

What Can You Make With a Cricut Machine?

Now, we come to the truly fun part of working with a Cricut machine. When being creative with a Cricut, your only limitations stem from the type of materials the machine can handle and its installed features. Other than that, the shapes you'll create and the purpose they'll serve are left to your imagination.

Amazing Things You Can Create With a Cricut

Scrapbooking and decorations. If you want to make an amazing vision board, a scrapbook, or an inspirational poster, a Cricut is a neat tool to have since finished products like these can cost quite a bit. A Cricut lets you print and cut shapes, words, letters, or even entire sentences and quotes. With this in mind, you can use it for a cleverly designed organization panel or a vision board, to cut out meaningful quotes and add them to your journal, scrapbook, or hang them on a wall, and so much more.

Cards and envelopes. Whether it's a gift card, a letter, or an event invitation, the average Cricut has built-in operations that can either streamline the cutting and folding of shapes or incorporate beautiful prints and embossment for a finer look. Having this possibility in your own home can make your life a lot easier. From not having to run and buy envelopes, to the possibility of making personalized invitations for your child's birthday or even creating luxury greeting cards and business cards—the possibilities are endless with a Cricut machine. Plus, printing and sending family pictures to make holiday cards will save you major bucks. Ordering personalized products such as these can cost hundreds of dollars, but printing and cutting your machine costs next to nothing. All you need to do is grab your chosen type of paper, and you're good to go.

Home and accessories. Cricut can cut through smaller pieces of fabric, and you can use them to make easy baby onesies, leggings, and shirts. All you need to do is either create or download a pattern, let the machine do its work, and then sew in the fabric pieces knowing that they'll be just the right design and fit. The same principle can be used when making or repurposing linens, mats, or wall decals. Imagine being able to repurpose a worn-out T-shirt into a small pillowcase or a fine towel. Cool, right? Cricut machines also allow you to make your window decals, organization labels, banners, and buntings.

Interior design. Aside from cutting unique decorations, a Cricut is also ideal for making your painting stencils, picture frames, and quote artwork. You can also use it to make a matching pillow, sofa cushions, and other creations. With the help of a Cricut machine, you can effortlessly cut Christmas ornaments, party decorations, and even prints for glasses and mugs.

Jewelry. If you learn how to work with a Cricut die-cutter, you can also make your custom jewelry, like leather bracelets, custom earrings, pendants, and so much more! You can also make a custom pet collar, and do countless other DIY projects!

Business and office. A Cricut allows you to make your very own personalized, brand calendars, stickers, bullet journals, planner designs, and business cards. If you own a business or you're planning to start one, you can use a Cricut to put your brand name, logo, and business information on all sorts of promotional products, like keychains, mugs, coasters, and other items.

What Can't You Do or Make With a Cricut Machine?

Your projects will depend on the specific possibilities of the Cricut model you choose. That being said, there are a couple of general limitations that apply to all Cricut projects:

Printing. Your Cricut won't be able to print images. However, you can use it for pen writing and apply numerous pens and ink for drawing. This gives you the possibility to choose text, colors, font, and size for any writing you wish to put on paper, even though you cannot print exact images. Instead, you'll have to provide a layout with the chosen color, pattern, or image to cut in the desired shape and apply the writing. This entails some careful thinking when making your designs. Keeping in mind that any images you wish to include will have to be printed in advance, you can later cut them using a Cricut. This way, you can apply a chosen image or pattern in the form of a sticker or transfer it onto the material before you start cutting more shapes and writing.

Sewing and gluing. Your Cricut can produce pieces for your project and decorate them with the type of writing you choose if you pick a more advanced model. However, your project will require further planning when it comes to putting a piece of work together. This might sound mundane at first, but you can easily find yourself lacking tools, supplies, or time to finish a project if you rely on the machine too much.

Safety. Depending on your project's intended purpose, all safety concerns will have to be thought through in advance. The safety and endurance of your finished piece will have to be accounted for when thinking about the size and shape of your design, as it strongly depends on the safety and sturdiness of the materials you use. For example, if you wish to cut out children's toys, you'll have to make sure that your design doesn't feature shapes that can be easily broken off or swallowed or that are too sharp and pointy. Likewise, it is up to you to ensure that the materials you use are suitable for the final product's intended purpose. It might sound appealing to use a Cricut for home decorations or even cutlery. Still, equal attention is necessary when choosing the most suitable and safest materials to endure the strain put on the object you plan to create.

Quality. Like safety, your work's quality and life span will depend on your choice of materials. Decorative pieces might not require particular material pickiness. Still, suppose the objects you're making will have to be washed, folded, or handled frequently. In that case, you'd be wise to look into materials that are water and heat resistant, perhaps antibacterial, and even machine washable. Whether it's vinyl, leather, wood, or foil, it would be wise to make sure that your materials can endure a significant amount of distress to get the most quality use out of them. Don't worry, we'll get into the nitty-gritty intricacies of material choice further into this book.

You now know just how useful a Cricut can be. You learned that you can use a die-cutter for arts and crafts, make useful tools, create decorations and accessories for your home, make jewelry, and create gifts for yourself and your family—you can even create entire pieces of clothing! A Cricut also gives you the possibility to make your office supplies and promotional brand products—that is, if you choose the right one.

Since you know how a Cricut machine works, as well as what you can and can't use it for, it's time to choose the one that works best for you.

Tools and Accessories

What You Need When Using a Cricut Machine?

Some tools and accessories go with these machines, and they can all add benefits to your projects and make your life easier. Some of them are as cheap as a single dollar, and all you have to do is shop around. You may think that it's not worth it to shop around, but the important thing that you need to know is that the time you spend looking for a better deal could end up saving you a couple of hundred dollars and leave your wallet and budget intact. This is something that will help. We will go through the different tools and accessories to go with these machines and a description to help you see why you would benefit from them.

We will talk about blades because there are so many different options for you to choose from. The Cricut has many different blades, and they all serve a special purpose for your machine, and it can be confusing to tell which one you should use. In this book, we're going to explain the differences you have in the following blades:

- Engraving blade

- Wavy blade

- Debossing blade

- Perforation blade

- Scoring wheel

- Rotary blade

- Knife blade

- Bonded fabric blade

- Deep point blade

- Fine point blade

The fine point blade is a workhorse for the machine. This comes with a new Cricut machine, and you can use it for almost everything you're going to be doing. It's gold and the blades have a white rubber covering that is new if you get them from the company itself. There are many other options that you can find out there for cheaper. However, the places to buy them cheaper might not work as well, so you will have to do your research. The blades have a forty-five-degree angle, and it is used for both series of machines.

The rotary wheel comes with the Maker, and it cuts fabric while being too sharp, so you'll need to be careful. The blade needs to be replaced quite often if you missed a lot of material, and there is a kit to change the edge. If you buy them used, some of the Makers won't come with this blade, and you can't buy one anywhere else, so you'll have to call the Cricut Company, and they will send you one for free.

The next blades that we're going to talk about are the perforation, wavy debossing, and engraving blades. All four of these blades are new, and many people don't have them yet. They are available in full housing or a quick-change tip.

The wavy blade can cut a wavy line across your projects like the scissors that came out about a decade ago to cut wavy lines into paper and were such a hit among teachers and paper crafters. The perforation blade is great for cutting dashes for tear-off issues, and the debossing blade is going to work like a scoring tool on the Explorer machine, but it goes a little deeper. The engraving blade is just going to engrave into metal and other materials, but there is an important note. There is a list as to what this can cut as far as materials that it can cut, and it's a good idea to keep checking because even though we have a master list here the company does change it from time to time, so it's good to stay on top of it.

The scoring wheel is only for the Maker, and it's almost the same as the scoring stylus for the Explore machines, but there are some differences. The blade on this is very dull, and it can also come with a double scoring blade. The scoring wheel is the first of the blades to have the quick-change housing, and the bottom will pop off, and you can attach a new type of edge to it. If you have rapid change housing, you can buy the new blades' tip, which is a little cheaper than buying the whole system.

The knife blade is like having an Exacto knife that cuts leather, Balsa wood, and many more items. It is only for the Maker, and you have to calibrate this when you use it because if you don't the app will have to keep reminding you to calibrate it. You can adjust the cut pressure as well, but there's a warning that accompanies this. This is not something for a beginner to try, and it's not the first thing you should try. If you're having a problem cutting the material, don't change the settings without thinking about it first and trying other ways to correct this problem.

Cricut does not guarantee that it will cut a material, which is why we have said check their website as well to see if they've updated it or made any changes. You can also adjust the pressure of the materials but do not change the setting more than one at a time or two at a time. Another tip is to be extremely careful with the knives as you could get hurt, so make sure that you're as careful as you possibly can so that you don't hurt yourself.

So, the following tools are from the Cricut Company, and one of the things that you might want to get for yourself is a weeder tool. A weeder tool is one of the most essential tools you can have because while the spatula and the tweezers that the machine can come with are beneficial. The weeding tool is necessary if you're trying to lift vinyl off of your mat. People can use many different tools for weeding, and they all work to raise the vinyl from the backing sheet in a safe way so that the project doesn't get ruined and your mat doesn't get ruined. However, if you want a tool that's direct from the company itself you can use the weeder tool, or you can buy the weeder toolset because it has finer points, and it might be able to do more for you.

Some of the other popular tools that people use for weeding are a dental pick, but the handles may be uncomfortable, however, you can also use an Exacto knife, but you'll have to be very careful not to damage the project or cut yourself open. They also use an old gift card or a credit card, but you should be aware that this might scratch the project, so you'll have to be very careful with this as well.

The next tool that we're going to talk about is the spatula. The spatula is for lifting material from the cutting mat when you don't want to worry about tearing the fabric. The spatula will take care of this by lifting the material from the mat as easily as possible, and it can also be used with a scraper tool to keep the mat clean and debris-free. Cricut sells the scraper and spatula together for a very reasonable price as well.

So now that we talked about the spatula, let's talk about the scraper tool. A clean mat is essential for getting a good project done and ensuring that your material isn't moving around during the cutting. The last thing you need when you are spending a lot of money on the material is to have it move halfway during the project, and then you have to start completely from the beginning, and you wasted all that money. Other tools remove that issue, but the scraper tool is much faster, and it ensures that you have a nice clean mat. There are different sizes, but most people prefer the extra-large as it's easier to hold, and it's faster than the smaller one, which means that it can also help get the bubbles out of your vinyl.

Extra mats are always recommended because there's nothing more irritating when working on a project than realizing that your mats are no longer sticky. There are definite ways to re-stick your mat, and they can save you money, but just in case it is still always a good idea to have a couple of extra on hand just in case you need them.

The mats do different things for different projects, such as the following:

- The pink that's for fabric is, of course, only for fabric.

- A strong grip, which is purple, would be better for thicker projects like leather, poster board, or thicker card stock.

- A standard green would be for iron-on and vinyl.

- The light blue would be for paper and card stock projects.

They also offer an essential toolset that has almost every item that we're talking about it. The toolset includes the following items:

- Tweezers

- Weeder

- Spatula

- Scraper

- Scissors

- Scoring stylus

By buying this you can cut down on a lot of money instead of buying the items individually if you just buy the set instead.

A bright pad is great for many different reasons because it makes weeding so much easier. After all, it makes the cut lines much more visible, but if you have anything more than a simple cut, this is really going to help you out because you'll be able to see exactly where the lines are, and you could even use it for adapting patterns and tracing.

An easy press is great as well. If you're still using the iron for heat transfer vinyl, the easy press makes things so much easier than iron because there's no peeling after one or two wares, and it takes out all the guesswork of the right time and temperature as well. If you have space, you can get a real heat press for just a little bit more financially if you can afford it. Still, we would recommend considering a beginner heat press first, especially if you're doing anything in a big quantity or for commercial purposes.

A brayer tool is good for larger vinyl projects or working with fabric, then you should use a brayer. This fixes the problem of not fully stabilizing your material before cutting. A brayer makes the material stick to the mat but without damaging it.

A paper trimmer is super handy if you want to get a straight cut. You do not have to use scissors, and you don't have to use a ruler. As such, it makes cutting a lot easier on you, especially if you're working with vinyl.

The company also sells their trimmer, however, there are other places that you can get a trimmer as well, and if you go with a shortcut paper trimmer, it has the option for scoring to get a perfect fold, so that may be something that you would want to look into.

Scissors make a world of differences well. The company scissors are made with stainless steel, which creates an even cut while remaining durable, as stainless steel is one of the most durable materials that we have. The scissors are quite sharp, and they come with a micro-tip blade, which means that working on the fine details in a smaller area is easier and clean right down to the point. It also has an interchangeable colored cap, which is protective as well, which means that your scissors can be stored safely.

The tweezers are super helpful, and many people have more than one type. They usually have one for small items and one for vinyl. This tool is in the Cricut toolset, but if you want to go for something else, there are Pazzlee needle point tweezers, and these tweezers have a very sharp point, which makes them excellent for vinyl. The points are also sharp enough that they can pick fine pieces from the mat without having to use the edges or any other little trick, and they can also pick up the tiniest little scraps as well. If you don't want to get the tweezers from the company, you can actually go with this other company instead.

Pens are a big part of the Cricut world as well, and you can purchase these pens in a variety of places. However, you can use other pens as well that you can find just about anywhere and for really cheap prices as well.

The other tools that you can get for yourself are if you find that you are a busy person and that you go to other people's houses or you go on business trips or things of that nature then you might need a tote bag to carry all of your Cricut supplies and machine. The company sells a great tote for a reasonable price that you would be able to use for your benefit and so that you will be able to keep everything organized and neat the way it needs to be. If you don't like their price point, there are actually a lot of other places that you can get a great tote as well.

You can also get rotary blades or a control knife. A control knife is basically like an Exacto knife, so you'll have to be careful with this because even though it adds precision and accuracy to your projects, you could end up cutting yourself pretty badly, so you'll have to make sure to be careful.

If you need rulers because you feel like you're not accurate enough, they have these as well, and they have all different types as well as kits that have all the tools that you need so that you don't have to buy everything individually. This is a great thing to look into so that you can see everything that you need. There are many different websites on the internet where you can find tools for your machine, and each boasts that their materials are better than the rest. Cricut offers everything that you would need on their site, and they offer very reasonable prices, but you can also do some additional searching if you feel like their stuff isn't what you would want, and you would want something else. As we've already listed examples from other companies, this will help you get an idea of what we're talking about. If you decide to get these additional tools, you'll find that your projects will be able to go a lot easier, and you'll be able to have more precision and more accuracy with them as well. Many people who like the Cricut and their company recommend getting these items for just that purpose.

The Best Materials for Cricut Explore and Maker

Materials That Can Be Used With the Fine-Point Blade

The materials in the section below all work splendidly with the fine-point Cricut cutting edge. Just change the pre-labeled settings on the dial or in Design Space to match what you are using.

Iron-On Vinyl

Iron-on vinyl is good for embellishing things that are made of fabric, for example, shirts, totes, fabric napkins, and so on. Make sure to use the iron-on setting on your Cricut. Iron-on vinyl (aka heat transfer vinyl, or HTV) is an outright favorite for many Cricut clients. It works admirably with a fine-point sharp edge. Generally, the standard grip mat will work with all types of vinyl.

There are different brands of iron-on vinyl. Read below to learn what the best iron-on vinyl is to use in your project.

1. Siser Heat Transfer Vinyl–Easy to weed, and they have been around for quite a while! Siser also has glitter vinyl alternatives, patterned vinyl, florals, and holographic choices!

2. Cricut Heat Transfer Vinyl–Cricut's vinyl is incredible. They offer a wide variety of colors and surfaces, like sparkles.

3. My Vinyl Direct–My Vinyl Direct also has types other than HTV so that I will point you back to it more than once. They have a lot of patterns, colors, and surfaces!

4. Firefly Heat Transfer Vinyl–Firefly is a widely known and trusted brand. In addition to the fact that it has extraordinary reviews, they too have incredible options! If you're searching for fluffy flocked vinyl or glitter vinyl, they have you covered!

5. Fame Heat Transfer Vinyl–This brand is good when you are searching for a wide choice of colors. The other advantage of this brand is that it is less expensive than some of the other options if you have a spending limit!

Adhesive Vinyl

Adhesive vinyl is a close match for the beloved HTV. There are endless uses for glue vinyl — for example, divider decals, mugs, decorations, compartments, wall art, and so on. There are two fundamental classifications of adhesive vinyl, permanent outdoor and removable indoor, with additional sub-types of both. For instance, removable glue vinyl would work best for a removable divider label, while lasting vinyl would work better for a wood sign you intend to place on your front door. For adhesive vinyl, you will use the vinyl setting on your Cricut. Use the standard hold function for adhesive vinyl. 1. Oracal Vinyl–This brand is my own top choice when I am doing an adhesive vinyl project. Oracal is viewed as the best at making vinyl by many people. This vinyl was proposed a year ago. You can purchase this brand from My Vinyl Direct in glossy or matte.

2. Cricut Adhesive Vinyl–Cricut is an incredible go-to asset for AV. Cricut has been increasingly more expensive, but there are times I need a specific shade or superior quality.
3. Expressions Vinyl–Expressions Vinyl is another beloved brand that is easy to use. They have a decent offering of glitter shades too!

4. Happy Crafters–you will discover vinyl of different kinds and a lot of other art-related supplies here!

Cardstock

Paper and cardstock are precious to me since I love to make paper flowers. Use the standard hold mat for cardstock paper.

1. Recollections cardstock–'Recollections' is a brand by Michael's crafts store, but they can also be found online! I use this brand the most for my papercrafts.
2. Savage Universal paper rolls–I recently discovered how magnificent Savage paper works for papermaking. Even though it is somewhat expensive, I keep using it because of its quality!
3. Paper and More– Paper and more is a trusted source. I love the interesting colors they have.
4. Cards and Pockets–This site has been around for quite a long time, and all things considered, the color choices are unmatched by most.

Additional Fine-Point Blade Materials

Here are some additional materials that use the fine-point cutting edge and the standard grip mat. For things like felt and leather, the fabric mat will be ideal. If you are cutting chipboard, sparkle cardstock, wood facade, or mat board, a standard mat will work fine. Rubber or magnets may require a solid grip mat.

Thin chipboard–Useful for wreaths or huge letter or number patterns. Set the dial to Custom and select Chipboard.

Thin poster board–Use for projects with foundations or enormous patterns. The dial ought to be set to a Poster board.

Stencil sheets

Sticker paper or tattoo paper–If you are using the print-and-cut component, consider doing it on stickers or tattoo paper. I like to cut my organizer stickers! Use the cardstock setting for these, too.

Vellum–Vellum is another type of paper that is typically fragile and translucent. It can be used in a variety of papercrafts. For vellum, set the dial to Paper or Vinyl.

Cellophane–Every once in a while, I find I need an adaptable and clear material. Cellophane works great for that! Cellophane should be cut at the lightest setting, normally paper or the one dot before it.

Materials That Can Be Used With the Deep-Cut Blade

For every one of the materials below, you will need to set your dial or machine to Custom and search the name of the material to set the best possible cut pressure. Specify in Design Space which one you are using on the cut screen. Configuration Space has a setting for a large portion of these alternatives in any case.

Chipboard–If you need thicker chipboard than the fine-point cutting edge can deal with, this is the time to put your deep-cut blade to work!

Rubber–Want to make your own stamps? You absolutely can with this extraordinary elastic and deep-cut edge.

Wood veneer embellishments–You may be able to use a fine-point sharp edge with wood veneer if it is sufficiently thin, but it is likely that you will need the deep cutting edge most of the time.

Magnets–Creating your own magnets can be extremely fun! They are fantastic teacher appreciation gifts, for example.

Leather–Leather is extremely popular today, particularly those awesome leather hoops!

Craft foam–Foam is superb for kid crafts. Pre-cut a lot of fun shapes and have your children enjoy some crafting time!

Matboard–Matboard is like basic cardboard, but nicer. So, whenever you need some matboard, it can work with the deep-cut cutting edge!

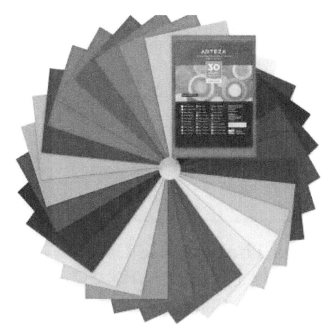

Felt sheets–Love felt flowers or artworks? Let your Cricut take the necessary steps for you! You can also do stiffened felt sheets!

Glitter cardstock–I love using my sparkle cardstock for a wide range of tasks. I have cut it with the fine-point sharp edge, but the deep one works better, particularly with the thick sparkle paper. Art stores regularly carry a few.

Materials That Can Be Used With the Fabric Blade

The fabric blade is pretty specific to the fabric. You will, to a large extent, keep the texture set up on the dial. Here are a couple of my preferred fabric stores to shop at. You may be able to cut fabric with the two sharp edges I previously talked about, but I suggest checking out the fabric planned cutting edge! I recommend using the fabric holds mat or standard grip.

Spoonflower–If you need A LOT of fabric to pick from or to craft your fabric in a couple of short snaps, then Spoonflower is the best option!

Joann Fabrics–Many of you presumably know about Joann's Fabrics. They have been around quite a while, and some of you may have a store close by.

Fabric Direct–If you need a major site loaded with fabric at discount costs, make sure to check out Fabric Direct. I have bought velvet from them for some fall pumpkin decorations, and loved the results!

Materials That Can Be Used With the Knife Blade (Cricut Maker Only)

With the knife blade cutting edge (this only works with the Cricut Maker), you can not only cut a lot of materials as you would with the deep edge but also cut materials 2-3x thicker than the Cricut Explore can deal with. The sharp blade edge can slice materials up to 3mm thick! More significantly, it does so with a more precise and cleaner cut than the deep cut cutting edge.

A new standard hold mat will work for materials thinner than 1 mm; however, as a rule, the blade cutting edge is used for thicker materials, so I prescribe the strong grip mat. If you're using something like 3mm balsa wood, you may likewise need to use some painter's tape around the edges to guarantee it doesn't slide mid-cut.

Settings: For wood, chipboard, and leather, there are settings you can choose by clicking on "see all materials" in Design Space. Specialty foam, for the most part, functions admirably on the thicker cardstock setting.

Thick balsa wood or basswood–This material is magnificent for wood casings, adornments, or assembling little items like a dovecote!

Thick leather–The blade edge has been praised for how clean it cuts thicker leather materials. So, if you need to make those great leather studs or possibly a satchel, then this is exciting! Perhaps you will be inspired by this gold and silver leather!

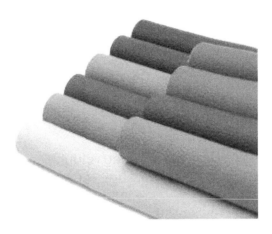

Thick chipboard–If you need a thicker chipboard material, the knife blade can take that.

Thick craft foam–Up your thickness with the knife blade by utilizing heavier craft foam!

Materials That Can Be Used With the Rotating Blade (Cricut Maker Only)

Mat to use–You can use a fabric grip mat for most light fabrics, though you can also use a standard or light grip mat for crepe paper and a light grip for tissue paper.

Settings–Delicate fabrics ought to be set to the fabric setting, while tissue, crepe, and washi paper require their own special settings (found under Custom Settings).

Washi sheets–Washi sheets are marvelous papers. They have a ton of fun prints on them. They work delightfully for cards!

Crepe paper–Can you say simple crepe paper flowers?!

Cork–Cork can be fragile to cut, so the rotating cutting edge is perfect!

Tissue paper–Cut tissue paper with this blade as well! Make it a point to pick a better-quality paper like the one here.

Delicate fabrics–Fabrics that are more sensitive, like tulle, organza and lace, are best suited for the sharp rotating edge.

How to Use a Cricut Machine

Setting up the Machine

First, you'll want to set up the Cricut machine. To begin, create a space for it. A craft room is the best place for this, but if you're at a loss of where to put it, I suggest setting it up in a dining room if possible. Make sure you have an outlet nearby or a reliable extension cord.

Next, read the instructions. Often, you can jump right in and begin using the equipment, but with Cricut machines, it can be very tedious. The best thing to do is to read all the materials you get with your machine–while we'll go over the setup in this book, if you're still stumped, take a look at the manual. Make sure that you do have ample free space around the machine itself, because you will be loading mats in and out, and you'll need that little bit of wiggle room.

Now, once you have the Cricut initially set up, you'll want to learn how to use Design Space.

Using Cricut Software

So, Cricut machines use a program called Cricut Design Spaces, and you'll need to make sure that you have this downloaded and installed when you're ready. Download the app if you plan to use a smartphone or tablet, or if you're on the computer, go to http://design.cricut.com/setup to get the software. If it's not hooked up already, make sure you've got Bluetooth compatibility enabled on the device or the cord plugged in. To turn on your machine, hold the power button. You'll then go to settings, where you should see your Cricut model in Bluetooth settings. Choose that, and from there, your device will ask you to put a Bluetooth passcode in. Just make this something generic and easy to remember.
Once that's done, you can now use Design Space.
When you're in the online mode, you'll see a lot of projects that you can use. For this tutorial, I do suggest making sure that you choose an easy one, such as the "Enjoy Card" project you can get automatically.
So, you've got everything all linked up—let's move onto the first cut for this project.

Imputing Cartridges and Keypad

The first cut that you'll be doing does involve keypad input and cartridges, and these are usually done with the "Enjoy Card" project you get right away. So, once everything is set up, choose this project, and from there, you can use the tools and the accessories within the project.
You will need to set the smart dial before you get started making your projects. This is on the right side of the Explore Air 2, and it's basically the way you choose your materials. Turn the dial to whatever type of material you want, since this does help with ensuring you've got the right blade settings. There are even half settings for those in-between projects.

For example, let's say you have some light cardstock. You can choose that setting or the adjacent half setting. Once this is chosen in Design Space, your machine will automatically adjust to the correct setting.

You can also choose the fast mode, which is in the "set, load, go" area on the screen, and you can then check the position of the box under the indicator for dial position. Then, press this and make your cut. However, the fast mode is incredibly loud, so be careful.

Now, we've mentioned cartridges. While these usually aren't used in the Explore Air 2 machines anymore, they are helpful with beginner projects. To do this, once you have the Design Space software, and everything is connected, go to the hamburger menu, and you'll see an option called "ink cartridges." Press that Cricut, and from there, choose the Cricut device. The machine will then tell you to put your cartridge in. Do that, and once it's detected, it will tell you to link the cartridge.

Do remember, though, that once you link this, you can't use it with other machines–the one limit to these cartridges.

Once it's confirmed, you can go to images and click the cartridges option to find the ones that you want to make. You can filter the cartridges to figure out what you need, and you can check out your images tab for any other cartridges that are purchased or uploaded.

You can get digital cartridges, which means you buy them online and choose the images directly from your available options. They aren't physical, so there is no linking required.

Loading and Unloading Your Paper

To load paper into a Cricut machine, you'll want to make sure that the paper is at least three inches by three inches. Otherwise, it won't cut very well. You should use regular paper for this.

Now, to make this work, you need to put the paper onto the cutting mat. You should have one of those, so take it right now and remove the attached film. Put a corner of the paper to the area where you are directed to align the paper corners. From there, push the paper directly onto the cutting mat for proper adherence. Once you do that, you just load it into the machine, following the arrows. You'll want to keep the paper firmly on the mat. Press the "load paper" key that you see as you do this. If it doesn't take for some reason, press the unload paper key, and try this again until it shows up.

Now, before you do any cutting for your design, you should always have a test cut in place. Some people don't do this, but it's incredibly helpful when learning how to use a Cricut. Otherwise, you won't get the pressure correct in some cases, so get in the habit of doing it for your pieces.

Maintaining Cricut

If you want your Cricut Machine to last for a very long time, you have to maintain it routinely. This means cleaning it properly and also maintaining the cutting mats and blades.

Maintaining the Cricut Machine

When using your Cricut machine, over time, it will inevitably collect paper particles, dust, and debris. Also, grease in the device will begin to stick to the carriage track.

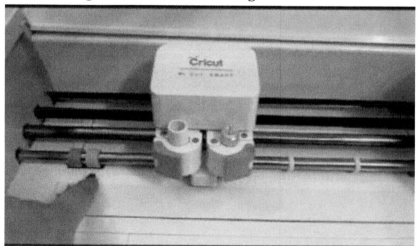

If you want your machine to last long, then you should clean it regularly, or else it can get damaged prematurely. Here are some cleaning tips to help you out when cleaning the machine:

- Before cleaning your machine, disconnect it from the power outlet. This will prevent electrocution or any other accident that can damage the device or injure you.

- When cleaning your machine, don't use any form of acetone. Acetone, like nail polish remover, will damage the plastic parts of the device permanently.
- You can clean the machine using a glass cleaner instead. Spray it on a clean, soft cloth and wipe the device gently.

- In the case of grease buildup on the carriage tracks, then you should use a tissue, cotton swab, or a soft, clean cloth to wipe it off gently.
- There is also the case of a buildup of static electricity on your machine. This can cause dust, debris, and particles to form on the device. This can also be easily cleaned with a soft, clean cloth.

Application of Grease for the Cricut Explore Models

- Disconnect the Cricut machine from the power outlet.
- Push the Cut Smart carriage gently to the left.

- Wipe the entire Cut Smart carriage bar with a tissue. The bar is the surface in front of the belt where the carriage slides on.
- Push the Cut Smart carriage gently to the right.

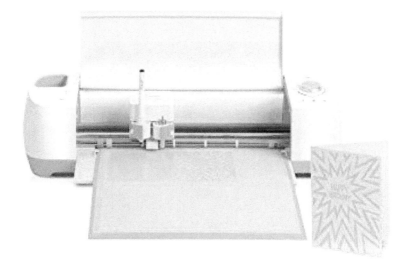

- Repeat the cleaning process for the other side by cleaning the bar with a clean tissue.
- Then, push the Cut Smart carriage to the center of the bar.
- Take a lubrication packet, open it, and squeeze out a little grease. Put the amount of grease on a clean cotton swab.
- Apply a small coating of the grease on the two sides of the Cut Smart carriage around the bar so that it will form a quarter inches ring on both sides.
- In order to make the grease become even in the carriage, push the Cut Smart carriage to both sides slowly and repeatedly.

- Clean off any grease that stained the bar while you were greasing the machine.
- You can purchase a grease packet from Cricut. This will work better than using a third-party grease packet so that the machine will not get damaged. This is especially if, after using another grease product, your Cricut machine is making a grinding sound.
- This process is almost the same as greasing your Cricut Maker machine too.

Maintaining the Cricut Cutting Mat

You also have to maintain your Cricut cutting mat because that is where the cutting takes place.
If the cutting mat isn't clean, it can stain the machine. Also, if your cutting mat has stopped sticking, it can spoil your designs and creations.
When your mat is no longer sticky because of debris and grime, cleaning it and making it sticky again will bring it back to life.
The solutions that I will mention are not ideal for the pink cutting mats, only for the green, blue, and purple.

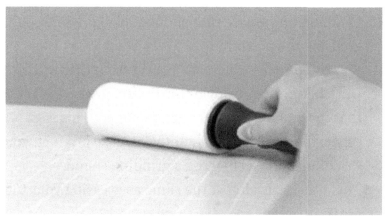

There are many ways to clean your cutting mat:

- Using baby wipes:

Make use of alcohol-free, unscented, and bleach-free baby wipes to clean your mat. You should use the plainest baby wipes that you can find so that you don't add lotions, cornstarch, solvents or oils to your cutting mat. If not, you could affect the stickiness and adhesive of the mat. Also, after cleaning it, let it dry completely before using it.

- Using a Sticky Lint Roller:

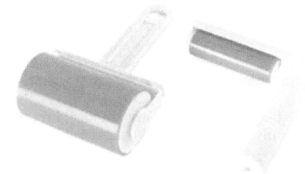

You can also use a roll of masking tape if you don't find a sticky lint roller. Run the roll across the mat to get rid of hairs, fibers, specks of dust, and paper particles.

This form of cleaning can be done daily or between projects so that dust doesn't accumulate on the mat. This is a fast way to remove dirt apart from using tweezers or scrapers.

- Using warm water with soap:

You can also clean the mat with soap and warm water. You should use the plainest soap possible too so that you don't mess with the mat. Use a clean cloth, sponge, soft brush, or a magic eraser. Also, rinse it thoroughly and don't use it until it is completely dry.

- Using an adhesive remover:

In the case of heavy-duty cleaning, then you should use a reliable adhesive remover to clean it properly. When using an adhesive remover, read the directions properly before you start.
Then, spray a little amount on the mat and spread it around with a scraper or anything that can act as a makeshift scraper.

Wait for a few minutes so that the solvent can work on the mat. Then, scrape the dirty adhesive off your mat with a scraper, paper towels, or cloth.
After this, wash the mat with warm water and soap in case there is leftover residue and let it dry properly.

How to Make Your Cutting Mat Sticky Again

- After washing or cleaning your cutting mat, you have to make them sticky again.
- The most advisable way to make your mat sticky again is by adding glue to it. Get a solid glue stick like the Zig 2-Way Glue Pen and apply it to the inner portion of the mat. Then, stroke the glue around the mat and ensure that there is no glue residue on the edges of the mat.
- After about 30 minutes, the glue will turn clear. If the cutting mat turns out to be too sticky after you apply glue, you can use a piece of fabric to reduce the adhesive by pressing the material on the parts of the mat that are very sticky.
- Cover the mat with a clear film cover after a few hours.
- You can also use tacky glues or spray adhesives that are ideal for cutting mats.

General Maintenance

- When your mat isn't in use, cover it with a clear film cover so that dust and hairs won't accumulate on the surface of the mat.
- Handle your mats with care. If you want to ensure that the adhesive does not get damaged, avoid touching the sticky surface with your hands.

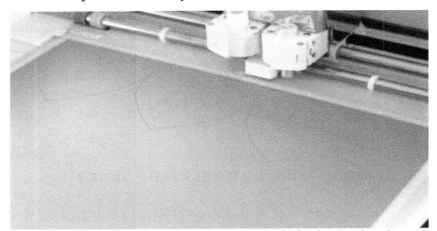

Always ensure that your mat dries entirely before using it or covering it up. Don't use heat when drying your mat, but you can place it in front of a fan. Also, ensure that it is drying hanging up so that both sides will dry.

Maintaining the Cricut Cutting Blade

You can use your Cricut fine point blade for over a year if you maintain it properly! The same goes for the other types of cutting blades. When maintaining your Cricut cutting blade, you have to keep it sharp all the time so that it does not get worn out.

Keeping your blade sharp is essential because if it isn't, it can damage your materials, and cause wastage. Also, if you don't maintain your blades, you will have to replace them often.

Keeping Your Cutting Blade Sharp

- Spread a portion of aluminum foil on a cutting mat. Without removing the blade from the housing, cut out a simple design in the foil. This will sharpen the blade and remove any paper particles, or vinyl stuck on the blade. This can be used for any type of cutting blade.
- In the case of heavy-duty cleaning, you should squeeze a sheet of aluminum foil into a ball. You need to remove the blade from the housing of the machine to use this method. Then, depress the plunger, take the blade and stick it into the ball of aluminum foil repeatedly. You can do these 50 times. This will make it sharper and also remove vinyl or paper particles on the blade.

How to Store Your Cutting Blade

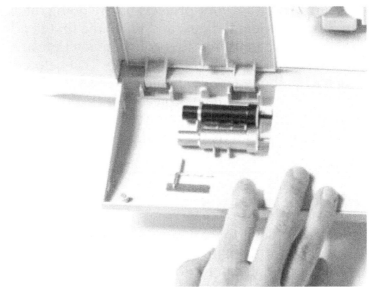

The best way to store your cutting blade is to leave it in the Cricut compartment. You can place it in the drop-down door that is in front of the machine. That compartment is meant for storing the blade.

As for the blade housing, you can place it on the raised plastic points at the back of the machine. There are magnets in the front of the machine where you can stick loose blades.

When you put your blades in the Cricut machine, you never lose your blades.

Problems related to Cricut Machines

Test those projects first! Testing is key to mastering the Cricut even when you feel like you've already gotten the hang of it. It never hurts to assess your projects before doing the final cut or print. It might seem tedious, and I'll be the first to admit that I'm very lazy where things that consume my time are concerned, but this really is a useful tip. Test before you cut. Make it a habit of yours. It should come without a thought. Instead of doing the whole project at once, do a small element of it first. If it doesn't work, you won't need to wait for it to finish before you can fix the settings and cut the new design.

Think of Fabrics

Fabrics are difficult to work with. Let's just get it out there in the open. I have given up on cutting fabrics completely. It's not that I don't think it can be done—I've seen people make wonderful fabric items with the Cricut—but I don't have the patience to sew so it is pretty much useless for me to try figuring it out. A friend of mine owns the Cricut Maker as well, though, and let me tell you, she is a beast when it comes to cutting the patterns and sewing them afterward! She made me cut multiple items that I just basically stuck together with a glue gun and it worked perfectly. It was much more efficient than doing it by hand. If you are looking to cut fabric, the Cricut Maker is your best bet. The Explore family is good for it too, but the range of fabric it can cut is limited compared to the Cricut Maker. Don't even look at the other machines. You're welcome for that little piece of advice.

Try Different Markers

Don't feel limited by the Cricut markers. That's right! When you are using your Cricut machine to write or draw on your project, any marker that will fit will work perfectly. Not only are there cheaper options but the colors and variety of styles are virtually endless. Don't let anyone tell you that you can only use the markers from the Cricut brand. Even though they are of better quality and actually made for the machine, you are not limited to using them. Just make sure your markers fit.

Double-Check the Settings

Just like the testers, this is annoying, but you have to make sure that all of your settings are correct and select the right material option. If you are not using the Cricut Design Space, this is easy to forget. When you utilize the software, there is a broad selection of tools to choose from. However, when you are only using a cartridge, the materials are limited. Still, regardless of which set-up you wish to handle the design, you should check your settings twice. If you are feeling paranoid (like I usually am), check them again just to be sure. It's easy to ruin a mat by not doing so. Trust me, I have lost more than one mat because of forgetting to inspect the setting of my machine.

Keep Your Blades in a Good Condition

As I have said before, buy extra blades. Preferably, get one for every material that you are going to cut. In the list of materials that are available to add to your Cricut purchase, you may see different kinds of blades available. For a particular item and that it is sharp at all times. A dull blade is never a good thing, and it will ruin your project as easily as a sharp one will cut it perfectly.

Extend Your Markers' Shelf Life

Keep your markers upside down with the cap-covered tip facing down when you are not using them. This will ensure that they stay nice and inky for the longest period of time. Do not leave them in your Cricut when you are not using them. Secure the cap and put them away afterward.

Peel the Mat Away

Avoid your paper curling by peeling the mat away from the paper and not the other way around. Did you wonder why I told you to do this when you were doing your project? This is the reason. Peeling the mat away from the paper will definitely ensure that your paper - or whatever material you are using - from curling.

Extras

Cricut has a complete cutting guide on their website, which makes cutting your materials easier. Reading that also reduces wastage of materials when you are testing your projects.
You can use Glad Press 'n Seal as a transfer paper to replace those expensive, original sheets. It is a cheap alternative that works well. The designs shift just as well as they would other materials.
You can use those pen grips that you don't use anymore to adjust a pen and allow it to fit into the pen grip of the Explore family and the Maker machines. Find them if you don't have any laying around the house. You can also utilize the grip of an old pen or even elastic bands to alter the size of the pen until it fits snugly in the unit.

We all know the Cricut mats aren't more than a tad expensive. So, what can you do when your mat loses its stickiness? Spraying your mats with Easy-Tack will instantly restore that feature and make it as good as new (or perhaps even better). Don't forget to cover the non-sticky edges when applying the adhesive to avoid having sticky hands and destroying your project too! I also made this mistake before, and I struggled to get the matt off my hands for half an hour. Moreover, I had to spend an extended amount of time cleaning the rollers of my machine because, of course, they picked up the adhesive and spread it all over. The apparatus also wasn't able to cut my project properly since the excess glue from the mat was making it stick to the rollers. It was a sad day indeed.

In that same breath, if you find that your mat is too tacky, you can always gently tap the mat a little to wear the stickiness out a bit or rub it on your clothes. Just be cautious of pet hair because that will not be easy to get rid of. If you do end up ignoring my warning and making this mistake, the lint roller will do a good job. It might not get all of it out, but it will help significantly.

If your blades are dull, and you need to stretch out their shelf life a little, crumble up a piece of aluminum foil until you have a proper ball. Poke the blade into the ball and pull it out again. Repeatedly do this technique for a while so that the blade will have extra few cuts in it. You can repeat this regularly to keep the blades nice. The sharper your blade is, the cleaner your cuts will be. This is a cheap hack with something that you already have at home.

Furthermore, you can use a lint roller to remove those little pieces from your cutouts that might just take you all day to remove by hand. It might not snag all of those pesky bits, but the tool will reduce the number of fragments that you will have to pluck out manually. This is also helpful for removing excess glitters from your project so that they do not fly around the entire house and give you headaches for years to come (yes, we all know terrible glitter is). As mentioned earlier, it is also great for removing hairs from projects as well as mats.

There are communities on social media that are great for novice and advanced Cricutters. You can ask any questions, and the members of the community will do everything they can to help you as they have been beginners too. Everyone is super nice in these groups, and you won't make a mistake if you decide to join any of them. It might be useful to have one-on-one conversations with people too since they might be able to help you more if they can personally interact with you and tell you what to do as you are making the project

Read the manual too. Oh, it's a tedious thing, believe me. However, it is important to learn your machine in and out before you start pressing random buttons. It will also tell you how to switch out your blades and insert the accessories in the new models; that's why it is super helpful. I didn't get a manual with the Cricut Cake as it was pre-loved, and the lady who gave it to me threw it away. It was a real problem for me to figure out what to do at the time, so make the effort of reading your manual. It will really, really help you.

Close up your Cricut when you are finished with it. I can't stress this enough. You should never leave your Cricut machine open for an extended period of time. This will allow dust—or pet hair—to make its way on the rollers or blades. When you know that you are done using your machine for the day, simply close the top and bottom lids to prevent unwanted gunk from sitting on your stuff. If you want to work with white material and there is dust on the rollers, chances are that it will transfer onto the paper, and you will have to clean the rollers before redoing the project.

CRICUT MAKER

The Ultimate Beginner's Guide to master
the cricut maker machine

Introduction

The Cricut machine is the last cutting machine released from the Cricut Company, which had already made itself known for the Cricut Explore, among others. The Cricut Maker is a plotter that can both cut various materials and write/draw on them. It can also perforate them (create those tear lines typical of cinema tickets, so to speak), engrave them (for example, Plexiglas and aluminum), create reliefs (such as in the case of embossing, even if in this house it is actually a debossing) or even folding lines (very useful if you make cards, tickets, boxes, etc.).

The machine will do one or the other depending on the accessory (blade, tip, or pen) that we are using. This machine is the Rolls Royce of cutting machines. And for a good reason! Imagine any media up to 3mm thick; the machine will cut it with ten times the power of the Cricut Explore and its other competitors. What made me fall for this machine is the possibility of cutting leather.

The Cricut machine can cut cardboard, balsa, vinyl, flex, burlap (!)... and fabric. Yes! You read that right fabric! And not just cotton! In the Design Space, you can find all kinds of fabrics: velvet, jersey, silk, lace! In all, the Maker cuts around 100 different materials up to 3mm thick. Another important feature of the Maker: you can write with it!

Whatever the type of material we want to work with the maker (paper, wood, jeans ...), we will have to introduce it in the machine after making it adhere to special reusable mats. These mats are equipped with a more or less resistant layer of glue: if we are using paper, we will employ a mat with a layer of not very resistant glue; if instead, we are using wood, we will use a mat with a much more powerful layer of glue. There are four mats available:

1) Light blue (Light Grip Mat), ideal for standard paper, light cardboard, and parchment

2) Green (Standard Grip Mat), suitable for heavy cardstock, printed paper, vinyl, and iron-on vinyl.
3) Purple (Strong Grip Mat), to be used with special cardboard, chipboard, cardboard, and other heavy materials and
4) Pink (Fabric Grip) to be used with most fabrics, including cotton, polyester, denim, felt, and canvas.

The Cricut machine has a double carriage allowing two operations to be carried out in a single pass. It is thus possible to draw (or use the "scoring tool "to make folds) and cut at the same time.

As on the Cricut Explore, an optical drive allows for Print & Cut. This has, however, been improved because it is now possible to perform a Print & Cut on colored or patterned paper.

As Cricut now favors the sale of patterns online, the Cricut Maker does not have a port to use pattern cartridges. To overcome the criticisms of their loyal customers, the American brand has designed a USB adapter (sold separately) to import the patterns of the cartridges into the Design Space software. The machine does not have an LCD screen, which can be confusing at first. But, considering that this one only displayed little on previous machines, users might think that the machine was limited to these few uses. The engineers at Cricut, therefore, decided to remove the screen to show that this machine was not limited in terms of capacity.

Cricut also emphasizes the unlimited potential of the Cricut Maker as well as its scalability. Indeed, the machine should accept in the future all future accessories that Cricut will market.

In terms of storage, we can note 2 locations for storing unused blades, pencils, or other small accessories.

You will never feel like you are limited by this machine because of the many possibilities it is able to offer you. The price can be a drag for some; however, this is a tough and versatile machine that you will keep for a long time. We must therefore consider this as a long-term investment. The Cricut Maker is a machine that you will not disappoint and that you will use for many years to come.

So, let's discover more about Cricut Maker, its tools, and its potentialities! And if you like this book, please leave a review after finishing it.

Cricut Explore Air 2 vs. Cricut Maker

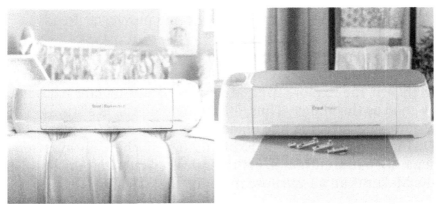

When the Cricut Maker was introduced to the public in the summer of 2017, one of the buzzing questions was; how does it compare to the Cricut Explore Air 2?

It's a valid question because the Cricut Explore 2 (a fantastic machine) had just been released as well and is, by all standards, a fantastic cutting machine.

The truth is that both are excellent stand-alone machines that are extremely efficient at what they are designed for; however, there are pros and cons associated with both, and each crafter will be more suited to either one.

The fight between the Cricut Maker and the Explore Air 2 is on, and this is an opportunity for you to examine the right choice of cutter for you closely.

Below are some comparisons:

1. Versatility

In terms of versatility, there's only one winner—The Cricut Maker!

The Cricut Maker does 100% of what the Explore Air 2 can do and even more. It consists of an adaptive tool system that can cut over 100 different materials and a huge library of sewing patterns. When you consider all this, you'll realize that the Cricut Maker is versatile enough to work with a variety of tools—including all types of blades released by Cricut, the brand-new knife, rotary blades, and the yet to be released ones as well.

You don't have to look any further because the rotary blade that comes with the Cricut Maker during purchase already puts it above the Explore Air 2.

The blade needs no supporting or backing material because it easily cuts through all types of fabric.

In theory, the Explore Air 2 is capable of cutting fabric but not as good as the Maker. Thus, a backing material is always required because the fine blade often catches on the fabric. Furthermore, users of the Explore Air 2 machine always use separate fabric cutters to get their desired cuts, but in contrast, the Maker is an all-purpose machine that does it all.

2. Cutting Specs

When we talk about cutting specs, we are referring to the machine that cuts best. Besides, cutting is the reason why people even go out to buy the machine in the first place.

If you consider the price (entry-level price) of the Cricut Explore Air 2, you'll agree with me that it is extremely cost-effective. The machine remains one of the best cutters around because its German-made carbide blade cuts through materials with extreme ease, and that's why it is used to make designs that are small and intricate.

In contrast, the Cricut Maker comes with blades that aren't only sharp and precise, but also possess a lot more force behind them, it has about 4,000 grams of force, whereas the Explore Air comes with a paltry 400 grams only.

The Cricut Maker cuts easier and neater requires fewer passes on thicker materials, and can work with way more materials than the Explore Air. Furthermore, the Marker is designed to potentially work with newer and sophisticated blades (such as the knife blade and rotary blade), as opposed to the Explore Air.

In terms of fabric cutting, the rotary blade remains a revolutionary invention that has greatly improved the industry, however, the knife blade has proven to be safer and more effective—it is the ultimate tool for cutting thick materials.

The Explore Air 2 is a highly efficient cutting machine that is perfectly suited for crafters that stick to thin materials, and do not require any special intervention.

The maximum cutting size of both machines is 12" wide by 24" long, and most industry experts are of the view that the Maker's cut size should have been increased to at least the size of the Silhouette Cameo 3 (12" wide by 10' long).

3. Price

It is obvious that the Cricut Maker is an improved version of the Explore Air 2; however, many people agree that those improved features fail to justify the hike in price.

The Cricut Maker is listed at $399.99 on the Cricut website, and although it comes with improved features, many people see it as a significant amount to lay down on a cutter.

On the other hand, the Explore Air 2 is listed at $299.99 and during sales, the price drops down significantly.

4. Longevity

Generally, when people weigh their options for products they intend to purchase, most times, they consider price ahead of other factors, but the truth is that price isn't everything. Thus, another factor to look out for is the products' longevity.

In terms of longevity, the Cricut Maker and the Explore Air 2 are very solid machines and there's absolutely no doubt about their durability. However, the Maker seems to be more suited for the future because the cutter will ultimately outlive more than the Explore Air 2.

Besides, the Cricut Maker comes with the Adaptive Tool System, meaning that it is guaranteed that it'll be compatible with all types of blades and tools that will be released in the foreseeable future.

No matter how much the crafting process evolves over the next couple of years, the Cricut Maker will remain effective and relevant.

On the other hand, the Explore Air 2 is not designed to offer more than it already does, and although it won't become obsolete, it just can't support the newer blades and tools that are being released by Cricut.

In comparison, the Explore Air 2 is meant for people that are happy with their available options and are concerned about upgrading their skills, whereas the Cricut Maker is suitable for people that intend to experiment and develop their crafts further.

5. Software

In terms of software, there's nothing that separates these two machines because they both use the Cricut Design Space software.

Design Space Software is a decent program that is easy to use and contains plenty of editing options for users to personalize their designs effectively.

Users can upload their designs and convert them free of charge; thus, expert users can create their complex designs in more sophisticated programs like Adobe Illustrator, Corel Draw, Make the Cut, and Sure Cuts A Lot.

Cricut Design Space is cloud-based so that users can design on their personal computers, tablets, and phones.

It is a user-friendly program, but it has its flaws: sometimes, it gets buggy and limiting, especially while creating new designs within the program.

6. Sewing Projects

In terms of the usage for sewing projects, it's not a contest! The Explore Air 2 is a versatile machine, but it doesn't measure up to the Cricut Maker.

On the other hand, apart from the actual sewing machine, the Cricut Maker is what people use for serious sewing projects. The Maker comes with a library that contains plenty of sewing patterns, and it not only cuts the patterns, it also marks them with the washable fabric marker pen. The Cricut Maker eliminates guesswork regarding the marking of patterns, which ultimately improves the final output of the work.

7. Portability

One of the most important but often overlooked features of machines is portability. If you're a crafter that prefers to be static, then you can overlook it, but if you're someone who prefers to travel with your cutting machine, then you have to consider the size of the machine.

Between the two machines, the Cricut Maker is the heaviest, weighing almost 24 lbs. as against the Explore Air 2 that weighs only 14.8 lbs.

The Cricut Maker is a static machine specifically designed for use in a specialized space, home, or craft room. It has plenty of storage space and even comes with a provision for charging phones and/or tablets.

The Explore Air 2 is nimble and it comes with a smaller amount of storage; thus, it is perfect for people that like to craft on the road.

In terms of portability and ease of movement, the Explore Air 2 stands taller than the Cricut Maker.

8. Ease of use

Both machines are relatively easy to use with little practice, but in terms of ease of use, the Cricut Maker edges the Explore Air 2.

The Explore Air 2 is built with the Smart Set Dial on the front and this allows users to select from the most common materials easily. Once the dial is set, the machine automatically adjusts its cut settings accordingly.

However, the problem most users face is that most of the materials the cutters use are not always the most common materials for members of the larger Cricut community. Thus, you have to manually set the material settings from within Design Space if your material isn't on the dial.

It is not an extremely difficult process, but it is a bit frustrating, especially when you have to carry out the same procedure over and over again.

On the other hand, the Cricut Maker automatically adjusts its settings according to the type of material that is loaded on the cutting mat.

It is extremely easy, and the user doesn't have to do any settings at all.

9. Cartridges

Newcomers in the world of Cricut and the cutting of crafts might not understand this; however, long-time Cricut users will know all about the cartridges—they might even have a space dedicated to them in their craft rooms.

It is no longer mandatory to use cartridges for designs on both the Cricut Maker and the Explore Air 2.

However, in case you have a couple of old cartridges at home, you might want to use them; thus, you can plug them directly into the Explore Air 2, and use them.

It is possible to use the cartridges with the Cricut Maker, but it is a bit more complex. You will have to get the cartridge adapter that will allow you to link the physical cartridges into Design Space. The cartridge adapter uses a USB port to connect the Cartridges with the Maker.

There is also the option of using digital cartridges instead of buying the adapter. These are downloaded directly into Design Space.

10.   Print Then Cut

The last and final battle between the Explorer Air 2 and the Cricut Maker is which of the machines have a better Print Then Cut.

The Cricut Maker comes with the Print Then Cut (PtC) feature, which allows users to print out their designs onto a white paper and then cut.

This feature comes in handy for crafters that tend to experiment more on new designs, as opposed to just downloading designs from Cricut Design Space.

The Explore Air 2 also has the same PtC feature as the Cricut Maker; however, the difference is that the Cricut Maker can PtC on colored and patterned paper, while the Explore Air 2 can't.

Thus, in terms of PtC, the Cricut Maker edges the Explore Air 2.

Overall Verdict

At this point, it is obvious that the Cricut Maker is the superior machine.

It is more durable, offers better Print Then Cut functionality, easier to use, more versatile, and an all-around better cutter.

The Explore Air 2 is a very good machine that has served crafters for some time now and will continue to do in the future; however, the Cricut Maker is just too good for it.

The Explore Air is the perfect machine for crafters that use paper, thin materials, cartridges, and also those that have a limited budget.

Both machines are highly efficient, and they serve their purposes perfectly; the Cricut Maker is for makers, while the Explore Air 2 is for cutting crafters.

Machine Setup and How to Prepare the Material

How to Set Up a Cricut Machine?

Using a Cricut machine is an effortless task and does not require a lot of effort. It is not heavy and can be easily placed on a desk or a crafting table. The computer which you will use should have the Design Space software installed. After purchasing a brand new Cricut maker, take note of the contents of the box. The device comes with the power cords, one mat, and a blade. Following are the instructions to set up the machine:

How to Plug in the Device?

First, the Cricut machine needs to be plugged into the computer and also the power outlet. Use the USB cable provided to connect the computer to the engine. Next to the USB cable, the power port should be connected to both the outlet and the device, also provided in the packaging. Now press the ON button on the machine. It will illuminate to indicate that it is working.

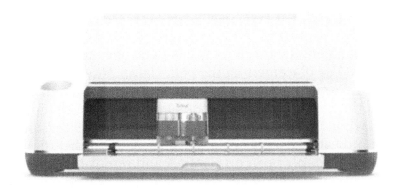

How to Load/Unload the Mat?

For placing your material to cut it on the mat, it is essential to know the placement. First, the mat's cover should be removed and placed elsewhere. The Cricut maker comes with a blue LightGrip cloth, which is used for cutting paper mainly. The match will be slightly sticky for proper placement of the material. When loading, the content should be placed in the top left corner of the mat. Be sure to press down gently so that the material could be evened out. Place the top of the carpet in the guides of the machine. Gently press on the rollers and press the load/to unload the button on top of the Cricut. Once loaded up, the software will tell you the next step. After the project has been finished, the material needs to be unloaded. Press on the load/unload button and take out the mat from the machine. The right way to remove the content from the mat is that it should be placed on a level surface, and the carpet should be peeled off. The remaining scraps can be peeled off by a scrapper or a tweezer.

How to Load/Unload Cricut Pen?

For loading a pen, the machine needs to be opened to show the two clamps. For placement of the pen, clamp A needs to be opened up. Remove the cap on the pen and place it so that the arrow on the pen is facing the front. Gently pull the clamp upwards when putting the pen. Place the pen inside the clamp until the indicator disappears, and a click sound is heard. To unload a pen, simply open up clamp A and remove the pen by upward motion. If you do not remove the pen, the machine will not be closed, and the pen's cap cannot be put on.

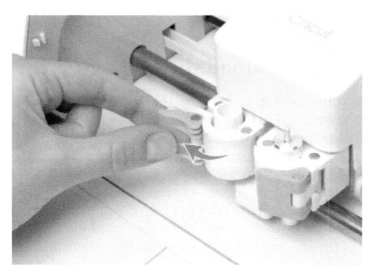

Recently, new specialized pens are available called the Infusible Ink Pen and markers. They work in by sublimation process, completely fusing the ink onto the material. It is best for Iron-on. The difference between it and regular pens is that they leave a thicker line. They also come in in two variations: traditional and neon. Heating is required to use this instrument, which can be achieved by Cricut Easy Press. For using it, first select a blank slot and fit the pen into it; any unused slot can fit the pens. Then draw your design on design space or by hand. Make sure the image size is according to the Cricut Easy Press. Then place a laser paper onto the Cricut Maker or Cricut Explorer. Now use the Infusible Ink to draw in the design. Now transfer the image to Cricut Easy Press and follow its guidelines.

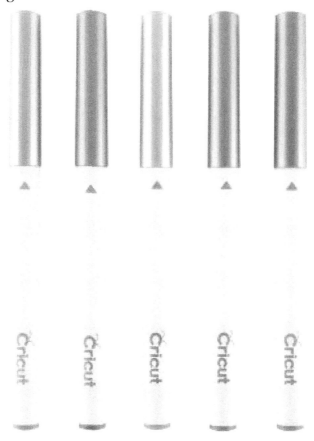

How to Load/Unload Blades?

A Fine point blade comes already place inside the machine when the package is opened. If the project requires a changing of the blade, then first, you need to unload the module. Open up accessory clamp B and pull it upwards gently. Then remove the sword from the machine. When putting another blade, i.e., rotary blade, make sure that the gears fit evenly. Once placed, it will give a click sound. Whenever someone is doing a project, the Cricut Maker automatically checks if the right blade is placed. With Quick Swap housing available, it is easier to change blades. Simply press on the housing tip to loosen its grip, and then slide or remove the leaves.

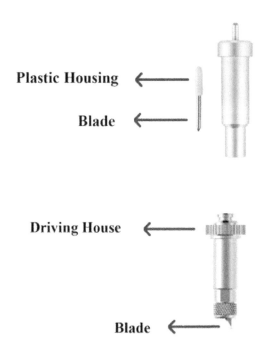

How to Load/Unload a Scoring Stylus?

To load and unload a scoring stylus is just as loading and uploading the pen. Open up the accessory clamp A and put the pen tip downwards, while holding up the clamp gently. Place it in until the arrow disappears, and a click sound is made. Now close the clamp and follow the instructions in the software. Once the scoring is completed, the scoring pen needs to be unloaded. Open up the clamp and remove the pen by pulling it upwards.

How to Load or Unload Cartridges?

Cricut Explorer comes with the feature of using cartridges. To use a round first, you need to open up Design Space using our Cricut account. Open up the green account button and click on the link cartridge option. A new page will open, which is the link cartridge window. Now turn on the Cricut Explorer and put the cartridge in the cartridge slot. The cartridge label should be facing forward, and it should be fully set. When the software air recognizes the round in the device, then click 'link cartridge' at the lower right corner of the screen. The screen will confirm whether the cartridge has been linked or not. Now the cartridge can be safely removed. To access the cartridges files, first, you should open Design Space with your Cricut ID. Then click on the ownership icon and select purchased. Now find the cartridge that you are looking for. To insert the items in your round onto a design, on the Design Space window, click on insert and search for the cartridge by name or click on the cartridge icon.

How to Load or Unload a Debossing Tool?

Debossing tool also called a debossing tip, is used to press on the materials giving it an everlasting imprint. Instead of a solid end, it has a rollerball which allows the color to slide onto the content rather than dragging on. This feature gives sharp images and opens up new possibilities. It is used in the Cricut Maker. It goes into the Quick swap housing and like any other blade into clamp B.

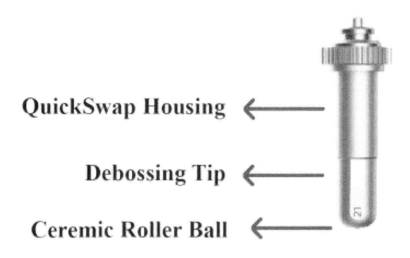

QuickSwap Housing ⟵ —————

Debossing Tip ⟵ —————

Ceremic Roller Ball ⟵ —————

How to Cut Vinyl from a Cricut Machine?

First, place the Vinyl liner side down onto the Standard grip mat. Then put it inside the machine after selecting the design. Push the go button to start.

For a smooth placement of the vinyl, you should use vinyl transfer tape. Transfer tape is a kind of pre-mask that transfers vinyl graphics to a substrate after being cut and weeded.

After cutting is done, remove the negatives of the image by a weeder or a tweezer, only leaving the wanted design on the mat. Now remove the Transfer Tape liner. Carefully with the sticky side down, place it on the mat with the design. Gently press to remove any air bubbles.

Whatever surface you want the design on, it should be clean and dry. Carefully place the vinyl on the surface and gently press it down. Remove the tap by peeling it off at a 45-degree angle. If it is difficult, burnish it by using a scrapper.

How to Cut Basswood by Cricut?

For cutting a word, make sure that it is not thicker than 11 mm. Use a sturdy grip mat for its cutting. Handle the wood carefully as the wood can be more fragile and more comfortable to break. Use a craft knife and a ruler for this project. Clean the wood or use compressed air to remove all the dust. Mirror the images on Design Space. Brayer can be used to provide adhesion to the mat. Remove the white wheelers to the side of the machine. Check that the wood is not under the rollers; otherwise, it can cause damage. Make sure the design stays inside the edges of the forest — test before cutting the project.

How to Do the Cricut Website Setup?

For accessing different features of Cricut, you need to create only one account on Cricut.com. This is the ID by which you can use Design Space, shop, post, and share.
To create an ID, you need to provide an email address, password, the first and last name, and the country you live in. Click on the sign-in button, and the sign-in page will open. On the bottom, there will be an option for signing up. Click the option and fill in the details.
To sign in, you need to click on the 'Sign In' link, which is on the top left corner of the account screen.

Install Cricut Design Space for Windows, Mac, IOs, and Android

For PC/Mac users:

To make full use of the machine, it is crucial to download the Cricut design space plug-in. By installing, new features will automatically be updated in your software. If you use more than one device, they need to fix it on all of them. The plug-in is installed in two steps

- First, clear browser history, cookies, and caches completely.

- Then, install by typing in the URL:

  http://www.cricut.com/design/getWinplugin

A prompt will open, click on 'Save File.' Access downloads from the browser and select Run, Install and Allow Access. A disadvantage for PC users is that the Design Space does not come with Photo canvas, 3D layer visualization, Smart guides, and Snap mat like it does in IOs.

But unlike the IOs and Android, it provides Cartridge use, Templates, Curve text, Knife blade cutting.

For IOs users:
There is an app for iPad users for Cricut Design Space. You only need to download and install it to be able to use it whenever. Open App Store, search Cricut, and find the Design Space app and download it. However, you need a Bluetooth machine to be able to connect with the Cricut device (only Cricut Explore air machine has Bluetooth).

For Android users:
A new app called Cricut Design Space Beta, which is available in Play Store. It has straightforward overview screens for designing and playing around with the features.

A significant disadvantage is that in the Android version, you cannot use the program offline as on PC and IOs. Many other features are also not available such as print and then cut, photo canvas, and snap mat.

After installing and creating your ID, a window will pop up, telling you about cricket access. During the first login, Cricut Access gives a 14-day free trial to its subscription. Once you are satisfied, you can buy the membership package. The Cricut Access icon will always be present in your account menu.

Tools and Accessories You Need to Work With Your Cricut Maker Machine

It is very exciting when you consider the number of fun things you can do and all the supplies you'll have to get after purchasing a new Cricut machine. However, as much as it is exciting, it can also be overwhelming. From iron-on to cardstock, to vinyl, and foil, not to mention the mats, accessories, and tools. If care is not taken, you can spend as much on supplies as you did for the machine itself.

Before you proceed to buy these tools and accessories, you need to, first of all, ascertain their roles and importance. Below are lists of the tools and accessories you need to work with your Cricut Maker Machine:

Cutting Materials (Cardstock, Vinyl, Iron-On, Etc.)

1. **Vinyl:** If you intend to make stickers for cars, signs, tumblers, and coffee mugs, you'll need the following products:

    - Printable Vinyl: Mainly used for making stickers

    - Glitter Vinyl: Removable vinyl with sparkle

    - Holographic Vinyl: It is the same as basic vinyl but comes in different colors depending on the angle that is being viewed

    - Chalkboard Vinyl: Mainly used for making calendars and for labeling

    - Removable Vinyl: Mostly used for temporary items that are not meant to last long, e.g., for rentals and others

- Permanent Vinyl: Used for projects that are intended to last long

- Dry Erase Vinyl: Used mainly for labeling

- Stencil Vinyl: Used for making screen-print shirts or hand-printed signs

- Patterned Vinyl: Used for fun design projects like Star Wars, Mickey Mouse, Minnie, watercolor, etc.

Some other items include:

- Adhesive Foil: It is similar to vinyl. However, it is more complicated to use, thus, if you're new to working with vinyl, you should stick to basic vinyl for a start.

- Transfer Tape: You need the tape to get your vinyl from the backing to your project.

2. **Iron-On**: This is used to apply on hats, pillows, shirts, etc.

- Iron-On Designs: These are pre-made designs that can be used alone or customized with other types of iron-on

- Foil Iron-On: Used to add shine to your projects

- Glitter Iron-On: Used to add sparkle to projects; very easy to apply and weed

- Mesh Iron-On: Used to make jerseys

- Sport Flex Iron-On: Stretchy iron-on used for athletic wears

- Holographic Iron-On: Used to add dimension to projects, either with holographic sparkle or opal holographic

- Everyday Iron-On: They can be used for most projects! They come in different bundles colors and are highly versatile

- Patterned Iron-On: Used for creative designs like Star Wars, Mickey and Minnie, cute hippos, and watercolor. Basically, it is used to add fun designs to projects

3. **Felt**: Used for making ornaments, finger puppets, headbands, and dress-up masks.

4. **Cardstock**: Used for scrapbooking, making gift boxes, gift bags, and cards.

5. **Genuine Leather**: Used for making home décor, accessories, and more.

6. **Fabric**: Normally used for sewing projects.

7. **Faux Leather**: Used for making baby moccasins, key chains, windows, and fringe.

8. **Infusible Ink**: Used to create bold and permanent designs with pens and transfer sheets on the Cricut blanks including totes, shirts, coasters, and more.

9. **Window Cling**: Used for short-term projects for fridges, windows, and other appliances.

Accessories (Pens, Tools, Mats, Etc.)

1. **Mats**: They come in two sizes; 12x24 and 12x12, and it is advisable to own at least one of each size. You will have to choose the type of mat to use, depending on the materials you will be cutting.

- Fabric Grip (Pink): used for fabric

- Light Grip (Blue): used for cardstock and paper projects

- Strong Grip (Purple): used for thick cardstock, poster board, and other thick materials

- Standard Grip (Green): used iron-on and vinyl

2. **Pens**: They are used for making gift tags and bags.
3. **Tools**: They are not mandatory, but they can make your work much easier if you have them:

- Scissors

- Scraper: Used to apply transfer tape on vinyl

- Spatula: Used to remove materials from the mat

- Weeder: Used to remove vinyl

- Bayer: this tool is used in ensuring that the fabric lays flat on the cutting mat

4. **Precision Hand Tools**: These are tools used during projects, especially after you've cut and weeded your projects.

- Acrylic Ruler: Used to cut straight lines and measure fabrics and other materials.

- Self-Healing Mat: This is a double-sided mat used for sewing, vinyl, iron-on or even paper project.

- True Control Knife: Used to easily cut thick, thin, delicate, and brittle materials. It is used to cut large sizes of fabric down to size mats.

- Cutting Ruler: This is a very large 18" ruler used for obtaining straight lines with cuts and placing designs on your blanks.

Specific Blades and Tools for Cricut Maker

1. **Rotary Blade**: It is included in the pack when you purchase the machine. The blade is used for cutting fabrics.
2. **Knife Blade**: It is used for cutting thick materials such as leather, basswood, balsa wood, chipboard, etc.
3. **Scoring Wheel**: It is used to make clean and crisp score lines.

Extras (Easy Press, Totes, Bright Pad)

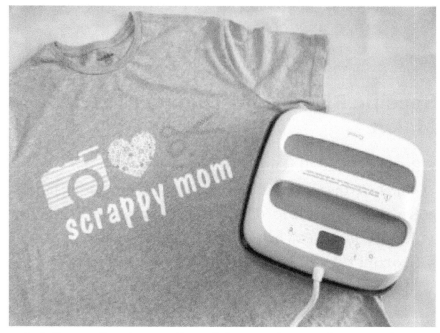

1. **Bright Pad**: It is a tool used for weeding and a must-have for people that plan on using plenty of glitter or even those that work in low-light areas.
2. **Easy Press Mat**: They are best used when applying iron-on. They trap the heat in materials so that iron-on can last long.
3. **Easy Press & Easy Press 2**: Are easy to use, portable heat presses. You need this item if you're going to be using a lot of iron-on. However, there's a slight difference between the Easy Press and the Easy Press 2.
4. **Storage Totes**: They are used for organizing, safeguarding the machine and other supplies. Below are three types of totes:

- Machine Tote: Used to hold cords and machines

- Rolling Storage Tote: Used to hold tools, Easy Press, laptop, Shuttlebus, cutting tools, and more

5. **Easy Press Totes**: Used to hold Easy Press machines, accessories, and other materials.

How to Clean a Cricut Maker

When the Cricut Maker was released by Cricut, it came with a new mat—the pink Fabric Grip mat. We all know that the Cricut Maker is a specialized machine for cutting fabric (among a host of other materials) and in order to ensure perfect fabric cuts, the mat has to be in top shape.
A lot of crafters find it difficult to keep their pink mats clean because it is different from the other mats used by the Explore Air series.

Do Not Use the Scraper

With the pink Fabric Grip mat, there is no need to use the scraper because the adhesive on it is totally different from the others and can be scraped off the mat.

Keep Your Hands Off

Unlike other mats, the Cricut pink mat is made with delicate adhesive. Thus, if your hands are oily, they can easily break down the adhesive on the mat, resulting in the loss of its stickiness.

Be very careful with the mat and try as much as possible to avoid touching the adhesive. To adhere your fabric to the mat, use a Brayer and do not apply too much force, just enough to get you to stick to the mat. Another way of keeping your hands off the mat is by using tweezers to pick up pieces of materials from it. Desist from picking up a loose thread from the mat too—use tweezers, if you really must pick.

Threads Don't Matter

Talking about threads, whenever you cut the fabric, you'll realize that you end up with a lot of threads on the mat. Leave them. In our minds, we believe that our mats have to be super clean because any form of a bump when cutting vinyl or paper can be detrimental to our project. However, the rotary blade is super awesome; it can cut through loose threads, even if there is fabric over it—the cut won't be ruined at all.

Transfer Tape

If you are really worried about threads or maybe they are affecting your cuts, then you can opt to use transfer tape to take off the loose threads and other debris. Just place the sticky side down and peel it up. This option doesn't work all the time, so you're advised to use it with caution, and especially as a last resort.

Tips for the Felt

Cricut Maker cuts felt perfect. Thus, if you intend to embark on this operation, there are a couple of options available for you to avoid damaging your pink mat with fuzz. First of all, you can use the older green mats and take off your pink mat. However, the green mat should have some stick. It is better to gunk up the old mat than to gunk with the pink mat with sticky fiber. Save the pink mat for fabric.
You can opt to back your felt in transfer tape and stick that to the mat. You just have to peel it off after the cut. Depending on the material you're cutting, this option can be capital intensive because you'll be using transfer tape for every cut.

Pushing the Mat beyond Its Limits

As with every other thing, the Cricut mat has its limits. Thus, if you carry out a lot of intricate cutting with the rotary blade, you will realize that the mat begins to peel off. By default, the rotary blade wasn't designed to cut circles that are below ¾". Crafters that cut smaller circles than that even put further pressure on the blade and mat. Since the mat isn't designed to hand such pressure, it begins to peel off.

Do Not Re-Stick the Mat

On the internet, there are so many tutorials on how to re-stick the Cricut mat, and they involve the use of baby wipes, water, painter's tape, Goo Gone, spray adhesive, and many others. However, you have to understand that the pink mat's adhesive is completely different from the adhesive on other mats, and if you use any of those materials to re-stick it, you'll end up damaging your pink mat.

The pink mat's adhesive is designed to grip fabric but also release it easily. There is no viable method for re-sticking the pink mat. It is advisable to take proper care of your mat with the tips that have been given, as opposed to looking for means to restore a damaged mat.

Advancing With Cricut Maker

Thinking of buying a Cricut cutting machine but still not sure which model? With about two worthy machines currently available on the market (the Cricut Maker, and the Cricut Explore Air 2), are you having trouble figuring out which machine would be right for you? So, we've written this chapter to support you choose the right machine for your intended use.

Comparison Between the Cricut Explore Air 2 and the Cricut Maker

Here, you'll learn about the similarities between Cricut Maker and Cricut Explore Air 2. They have some points in common; however, Cricut Maker has some specific functions, which are sensational.

Let's check them out!

1. Integrated Bluetooth technology, eliminating the need for a USB cable, making your workspace freer and more organized.

2. They use the same software that until this date is only available online. It is called Design Space and is compatible with Windows/iMac and Android/iOS systems, which can be accessed through the address: design.cricut.com

3. For iMac/iOS systems, the files can be downloaded for offline use. However, this option is not yet available for Windows and Android.

4. The projects, cartridges, and images are on the Cricut Cloud, and you can access them through your Cricut ID.

5. Fast cutting and writing mode, which can be used in several files.

6. Cut, write, and crease 100 different materials, up to 1.7 mm thick.

Cricut Maker cuts materials up to 2.4mm thick. Below we'll talk more about that.

They have compartments to store the blades and tools.

Double cart:
• On the left side (A), we insert extra-fine, fine, or medium-tipped pens and the crease tool or pen.

• On the right side (B) is where we fit the blades with their proper supports. At Cricut Maker, the gear blades are also included on the B side. We will learn more about them later.

Discover the Cricut Maker Blades and Bases

Blades, pens, and crease tool compatible with both machines:

• Fine Point Blade; usually the standard blade, and can cut materials a thick as 1.1 millimeters.

• Bonded-Fabric Blade that has a pink color. Its function is the same as the Thin Point Blade; however, it has a different color not to mix. In this way, the cutting edge will be preserved since they should only be used in their respective material. It can cut materials up to 1.1 mm thick.

• Deep Cut Blade is a black blade that cuts materials up to 1.7 mm thick. However, if the material is very hard, like chipboard, it may not cut.

• Premium blade (Premium Fine Point Blade), which has a slightly golden color, can cut materials up to 1.1 mm thick. However, it has more outstanding durability.

• Fine, extra-fine, and medium-tipped pens. They are from Cricut itself, and you can find them in different colors.

• Crease Tool or Pen: accessory purchased separately to crease the designs.

The two machines also use the same cutting bases with sizes 30 x 30 cm and 30 x 60 cm. It is necessary to be attentive since each base is to be used with material.

Below, we explain to you which material should be used with each type of base.

• Light Fixation Base (Light Grip Mat): for cutting lighter materials such as thin cardboard and tissue paper, for example. It has a light blue color.

• Standard Base (Standard Grip Mat): Used for cutting heavy paper such as scrap and color plus papers, for example, vinyl, transfers, and adhesive papers, and more.

• Strong Fixation Base (Strong Grip Mat): Its color is lilac and was developed to cut heavier cardboard, glitter paper, magnetic blanket, fabric with a heat-stabilizing / stabilizer base, chipboard, among other thicker materials or that need a stronger fixation for cutting.

• Fabric Cutting Base (Fabric Grip Mat): in light pink, it is designed to cut the most diverse fabrics using both the fabric blade and the rotary blade (exclusive to Cricut Maker).

As you can see, the types of bases have been developed for each group of materials, so for your project to have the right performance, it is recommended that you follow these guidelines.

Ready! Did you see how much the two machines offer you?

How to Set Up Bluetooth with Cricut Maker

1. Turn on your Cricut Maker

2. Type "Bluetooth" on the Search and click on it

3. Click on the "Bluetooth and Other Device Settings" option that appears.

4. Next, confirm that the "Bluetooth" option is "Enabled." If it isn't, click to activate it.

5. Click on the "Add Bluetooth or another device" option.

6. Select the option where you have Bluetooth and wait. That's because your computer will automatically detect your Cricut Maker and also other devices that work via Bluetooth.

7. The Maker option will be displayed as "Audio" on the list. However, if there are more than one Cricut device available at that point, you'll have to identify them using your device's code located on the serial number tag beneath your Cricut Maker.

8. Upon requesting a PIN, enter "0000" and then "Connect" it.

9. Click "Done."

Ready! Your Bluetooth connection is set up!

How to Print and Cut with Cricut Maker

Let's start this with a sequence talking about the basic shapes because with them, you can create appliques, tags, stickers, or whatever you want to print and cut out.

However, this chapter focuses on detailing each step to enable you to make the perfect Print and Cut on your Cricut Maker.

How to go about it?

1. First, in the left menu, go to the "Shapes" option and create a basic shape.

2. After that, save the file by clicking on the "Save" option in the right corner of the Upper Dark Bar of your screen.

3. A field will open to name your file. After naming it, click on "Save."

4. Before we start, a super important tip: always look at the "Layers" panel in the right corner of your desktop. It will be beneficial for you!

5. Now, with the object selected, choose the option "Print" located in the Top Menu "Fill."

6. Next to the "Print" box, a square is now in the color of the shape. Click on it and switch to the "Standard" option.

7. When choosing the "Standard" option, a box with all the program's prints or that you have already downloaded will appear there. However, beware! In this panel, there are free and paid prints.

8. Therefore, if the payments are chosen, a purchase command will appear on your screen when ordering the cut.

9. Choose a print of your preference. It may take a few seconds to load; it's normal.

So, let's cut!

1. First of all, click the "Do" button in the upper right corner of your screen. Make sure, at this point, that your machine is turned on and properly connected via USB or Bluetooth cable.

2. Over here, Bluetooth is my favorite because it eliminates wires from my workbench. Best of all, it is already integrated into your Cricut!

3. This is the cutting area. Wait for the connection to the machine.

4. Notice a black border around the file. It is like a registration mark. Therefore, through it, Cricut will read the exact location where the cut should be made. This margin varies depending on the file size.

5. After the previous steps, click "Continue" in the screen's lower right corner.

6. Now it's time to send it to the Printer! Click the "Send to printer" button.

7. A new window called "Print Configuration" will open, and there are a few options:

- Printer: where you will choose the printer, you will use at work.
- Number of copies: set here the quantity you will need.
- Add overflow: this option is advantageous, as it automatically adds bleed to the file. (Always test whether your work will be better with or without bleeding.)
- Use system dialog box: this option is if you want your standard computer print window to appear so you can have it printed through it.

Tip: When choosing this option, after clicking on "Print" your print dialog box can be displayed behind the Design Space.

8. After everything is configured, click on "Print."

Cutting Settings in Design Space

1. After the printed file, it is time to configure the material for the cut.

2. For this material follow the steps below:

3. For those who have Cricut Maker, place the Smart Button in the "Light Cardstock" position.

4. When the "On/Off" button is blue, it means that you are connected to the machine via Bluetooth.

5. However, when you will cut materials that are not available in the Smart Panel, place the button on the "Custom" option and follow the steps below also used in the Maker.

6. For those who have Cricut Maker, click on the "Light Cardstock" option ordinarily visible on the main screen.

7. When you need to cut some material that is not on the main screen, click on "Browse all materials" and locate it.

8. Note that after configuring the material, the Cricut starts to flash the light for loading the cutting base.

9. With the material configured, it's time to place the paper on the cutting base, load the tool according to the orientation on the screen and load the base on the Cricut Maker by pressing the button flashing.

10. Press the "C" button that will now be flashing to start the job.

11. The Cricut Maker will read the margin around the file (scanning) and then start cutting. You can follow the entire process on the screen.

12. Ready! Your print and cut are done and perfect! Click "Finish."

See? It's as simple as that!

CRICUT DESIGN SPACE

The Ultimate Guide to Learn how to
Use Design Space at its best

Cricut Design Space (CDS)

What Is Cricut Design Space?

Cricut Design Space is the web-based program considered to be the backbone of the Cricut machine. It is on this application that you can access the thousands of predefined designs (templates) that you can customize to create your own custom designs or start creating you from scratch. This platform contains around 75,000 images, more than 800 pre-built templates, and around 400 fonts, giving you a wide range of options to choose from when it comes to creating your designs or customizing any of the pre-designed designs you will encounter on the platform.

Simply put, the Cricut design space is simply where the magic of design happens and access to this platform is why you need to sign up with an internet-connected device in the first place. Other things you can do in this space include uploading your JPEG and SVG images, customizing your fonts to your needs, and generally unleashing the creative genius in you.

How Does the Design Space Work?

It is not enough to know that the CDS is an important tool, you need to know how it works.

Navigating through the CDS can be a bit overwhelming, especially if you're new to using this space and Cricut. This is due to the many features found in the space. If you are not trained to use these features and to know what each one stands for, you may not be able to use the platform and you will see that you will be at a loss for what to do whenever you are about to create your designs or launch a project. In this section of the book, we'll take a deep dive into the CDS and help you better understand what it is and how to orient yourself.

The creation of your projects and anything you want to crop with your machine is done on a window called canvas. Consider your canvas as a place where you can make all the designs you will be doing. Just as the artist's painting canvas is where all the magic happens, the design space canvas is where you can create and work on every project you need to work on. Attached to your canvas are many buttons and icons that can create in you that sense of despair or the feeling that navigating the design space will be a herculean task. The truth is, once you can look beyond that claustrophobic feeling you get from looking at all the icons on the canvas, you will find that the design space is not as difficult to use as it seems.

When you log into your design space, you will be taken to the main application screen. On the home screen, you will see many thumbnail images. These are templates you can customize to create your designs, and as a beginner, you may want to start by trying this step. It may be a little difficult to start creating your designs from scratch, so the best move sometimes may be to start by customizing a template to your needs.

However, you can start a new project if you feel you have what it takes to do it right away.

When starting a project, the first thing you will notice is that the canvas has a lot of grids. Grids are the fine lines that separate the entire canvas into small boxes. While they may seem like they are of no use to you, that's not the case because these grids play an important role in making sure you create the best kind of project possible. The grids help you visualize the cutting mat and keep your work together as they serve as tools for calibration. With them, you end up maximizing your design space and getting the best you can. The grids are calibrated in inches and cm. You can switch between these calibration units, depending on what you are trying to achieve and the calibrations you have on hand.

With your design space and all the tools present, you can create projects from scratch, import some functionality from an external point, and customize the projects that appear on the home screen after logging into the design space application. A lot can be achieved using the application and always remember that this is where all the magic happens when it comes to designing projects.

This is what the design space and workspace splash screen look like, respectively.

Download and Install CDs for Your Android Devices

1. On this platform, CDS can be used as an application, rather than just a web-based application like on other platforms.
2. To get started, go to the Google Play Store application on your phone and open it.

3. On the main screen of the Play Store app, you will see a search bar at the top of the screen. Activate this search bar and search for the application you want to install (which in this case is the Cricut design space).

4. On the search results page, you will see this app as it appears as a white square with a green Cricut logo (C) in the center.

5. Next to the application, you will see the "install" button wrapped in green. Tap this button to start the app download and installation process on your device.
6. Once the installation is complete, quit the Play Store app and go to your phone's app list. Search for the newly installed application and launch it.
7. With the application running, log into your account (if you already have one). If not, you will be asked to register for the CDS. In any case, follow the directions that appear and you will be ready in no time. Navigating in this application is not difficult. All you have to do is follow the instructions and you will be registered immediately.

8. That said, all you need to do is start designing on the go. You are ready to use the application you just installed.

For Your iOS Devices

1. The application is also available for download and installation from the Apple App Store.
2. Launch your App store and search for the application you want to install. When you have found it, click the "Get" button next to it and wait for the application to begin the installation process.

3. Once the application has been successfully installed, launch it and you will be presented with options to start completing the setup of your machine or to move on to get an overview of the application.

4. If you are not trying to do any of these, you will see a large "X" in the upper right corner of this page. Tap it to be taken to the home page, where you will be asked to enter your details and start designing.

For Your Windows Devices

1. With the browser above your windows device, leave for https://design.cricut.com/
2. On this page that you have opened, click on "download." Depending on the browser, the screen will change.
3. When the download is complete, double-click the file you downloaded.

4. Depending on the brand and settings enabled on your device, a pop-up may appear on the screen asking if you trust the application you have installed. Click on the option that indicates that you trust the application and continue with the process at hand.

5. After this step, a configuration window will appear showing the installation progress. Please be patient and allow the application to install without interruption. When finished, launch the application and submit your details to log into your Cricut Design Space account, or if you are a new user, follow the instructions to register.

Sign in with your Cricut ID

Email / Cricut ID

Password

Enter your password

Forgot?

☑ Remember me

Don't have an account yet?

Create a Cricut ID

6. At this point, an icon for the application you have installed will automatically be added to your computer's home screen. This makes it easy to access. To make it easier for you to access this application, you can choose to "pin it to the taskbar." With these, you are ready to start using your newly installed software.

For Your Mac Devices

1. With the browser above your windows device, leave for https://design.cricut.com/
2. On this page that you have opened, click on "download." Depending on the browser, the screen will change.
3. When the download is complete, double-click the file you downloaded.
4. Drag the Cricut icon to the "applications" folder icon to start the installation process.

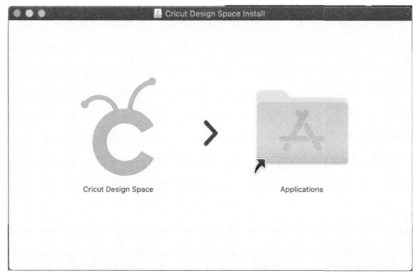

5. After the application has been installed, double click on the icon to launch what has been installed. A note may appear on the screen asking if you want to open the application you installed. Accept and wait for the application to start.

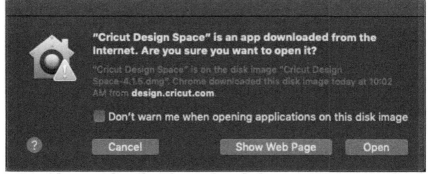

6. Provide your details (if you already have a Cricut ID). If you don't, follow the instructions to get started with this. After you are done, you will be redirected to the home page of the application you have now installed. You are ready to start creating your designs.

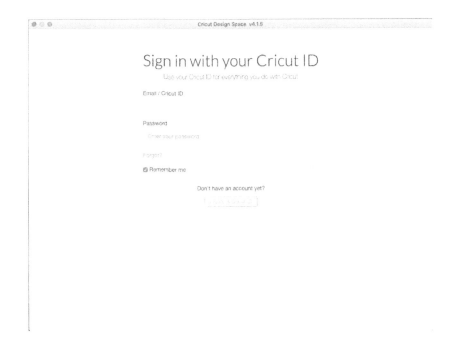

Sign in with your Cricut ID

Use your Cricut ID for everything you do with Cricut

Email / Cricut ID

Password

Enter your password

Forgot?

☑ Remember me

Don't have an account yet?

Put Your Cricut Design Space to Work

Cricut Design Space Canvas Options

The canvas of your design space is equipped with a ton of tools that can be of immense help to you, and when used efficiently, you can produce many designs that are amazing and out of the ordinary. However, if you're going to be successful while using your canvas, you need to be able to understand exactly what you'll find in your canvas and how to navigate this important part of Cricut's design space.

This is exactly what we will do in this section of the book. The design space canvas is where most of your project work takes place. Given the importance of this tool, we can easily divide it into four main sections including:

- The header

- The canvas

- Design panel

- Layers panel

All these parts have icons that are very useful for the Cricut design space canvas and we will take a quick look at them all, individually.

A. The Header

The header is the topmost layer of the canvas. It is similar to the home screen but has some features that make it unique in so many ways. When you start working on a project and have yet to save it with a name, the page name in this section of the design space will show "canvas." This is right in the MS Word simile, where the title bar shows "document" if you have yet to save what you are working on.

In the center of this section, you will see the name of the project you are working on as it is displayed in bold. On the far right of this section, you will see three buttons including:

- My projects; which allow you to quickly see the projects you have worked on and are currently on so you can immediately jump to projects.

- Save; which allows you to save what you're doing to a storage device with the click of a button.

- Just do it; which is used to send the instruction to your machine that a design is ready to be created. This is like the last step in the design process.

B. The Canvas

This is the creative space. This is where you can design, customize and edit your designs with the images, fonts, and personalization options available in the design space. Making use of the canvas is easy. It's just like space where everything you collect from other sections of the design space is cut out and edited.

As discussed earlier, your canvas is divided by grids and these play an important role in making sure your designs are executed as accurately as possible. The measurements on this canvas can be alternated from inches to cm. In the design space settings, you can also choose to turn off grids, leaving you with a plain canvas.

Editing on the canvas is relatively easy. Whenever you want to make changes to an element you've added to your canvas, all you have to do is click on the element and a blue highlight will appear on it. Any changes made at this point will affect the highlighted item.

There are many other options and they include:

- Deleting elements from the canvas. To achieve this, all you have to do is click on the red "X" button that appears in the design space. This removes any highlighted elements from the canvas.

- Freeze elements on the canvas. In the lower right corner of the screen, you will see a small button that looks like a key. This button allows you to "freeze" elements on the canvas. Locked items are not open to modification or modification, and if you need to change a locked item, the first step is to unlock it.

- The zoom effects. You can see the elements and design on your canvas in more detail without changing the actual size of your design. All you have to do is click on the little + and - signs in the lower-left corner of your canvas. This way, you can create more detailed designs as you can interact more closely with the elements of your design.

C. The Design Panel

The design panel is located in the far-left corner of the screen. It is a horizontal bar that contains the following features from top to bottom:

- The first button allows you to start a NEW project. When you click on this, you are transferred to a blank canvas and start working on something new.
- The second button allows you to open a PROJECT ready to be created. The third button allows you to customize your project by adding a file IMAGE.
- The 'Next' button is also an important tool for customization as it allows you to add TEXT to your projects.
- With a click on the Next button, you can further customize your designs by adding a SHAPE to the project in question.
- The last button in this panel allows you to UPLOAD your images, text, and personalization effects so you can incorporate them into the project you are working on.

With this toolbar, you can make more detailed changes to the projects you are working on. This tool allows you to undo or redo an action, flip an element on the canvas, arrange elements the way you want them to be, align elements, rotate, and adjust the position of elements on the canvas, among many other things.

D. The Layer Panel
This is the horizontal bar at the far right of the screen. The layer group has icons that allow you to do this:

- GROUP elements on the canvas. This allows you to perform a specific action on a group of items at the same time. While you would have taken individual action on several elements on your canvas, you can save yourself the stress by grouping these elements and working on them as if they were a unit.

- UNGROUP elements that have been grouped previously. This will bring them back to being individual units and then you can make changes as needed.
- DUPLICATE items. This function allows you to produce the same element again.
- DELETE items, just as the name suggests.

A few more options are available at the bottom of this panel, including "slice," "weld," "connect," "flatten" and "outline." These give you the freedom to do more with your designs, creating better effects with the click of a button.
This is what the interface looks like and all the panels discussed above have been highlighted on the next page.

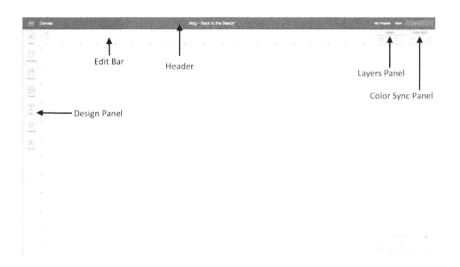

Troubleshoot Cricut Design Space Error codes

Error code (-2): This is an "Unsupported Error." This implies that the action you are trying to perform is not supported.

Possible solutions:
1. Make sure you try to cut with the right type of machine; Explore and Maker machines. Others are not compatible with the design space, and this can lead to difficulties when working with the design space.
2. Make sure you are using an updated browser. If necessary, make sure you have completed any other updates that you need to complete.
3. Verify that the system meets the minimum requirements for the design space.

B. Error code (-3): "Device already in use" error.

Possible solutions:
1. Start by restoring the connection. This attempts to update the connection between the device and the machine.
2. Complete the new machine setup process or you will not be able to get past this error code.
3. Disconnect the machine from the device and restart it. Also, restart your computer and reestablish the connection.
4. If possible, exchange connection tools; use the Bluetooth connection if you were using a USB cable and vice versa.
5. Contact design space member support for assistance if none of these helps.

C. Error code (-11): "Device authentication" error. This can be the result of programs running in the background.

Possible solutions:
1. Make sure you are using an updated browser.
2. Stop applications running in the background.
3. If these do not work, disconnect the machine from the device and restart them.

D. Error code (-21): "Data transmission error"

Possible solutions:
1. Clear browser history. Remove caches and clear cookies.
2. Restart your browser and try cutting again.
3. Check your Internet browsing speed and the strength of your signals. This could be a problem and if you see there are difficulties here, you may want to wait until the signal is better or switch to another service provider.

E. Error code (-24): "Ping timeout" error.

Possible solutions:
1. If you are facing this challenge with a project, it could mean that the project is too big. Recreate the project.
2. Change the connection tool you are using. Swap USB cables, if possible, or USB to Bluetooth and vice versa.
3. Check your internet speed. It may not meet the minimum requirements of 2 Mbps for download and 1.0 Mbps for upload.

F. Error code (-33): "Invalid material setting" error.

Possible solutions:
1. Check the settings of the material you are using. If it is set to "custom" and no material is selected, this could be the cause of this design error you are getting. All you have to do at this point is selecting the material you want to use.
2. If you still receive this error report after changing your material setup, please contact enrollment support.

How to Use Design Space?

What Is the Cricut Design Space Menu?

First, open up the Cricut account by signing in with your Cricut ID or make a new account by clicking the sign-up.

The design space menu will open up; it is the screen where anyone can manage their set up. You can browse the menu. Clicking on the home button will bring the Home page up. By clicking, the current project is not lost. By clicking on Canvas, the site takes you to the Canvas window. Here you can design a new project. If you are working on a design, it will directly open to it. There is an option for print in cut calibration for accurate cutting of images.

A new machine can be set up by clicking on the new machine setup button. If the machine needs an update on its Firmware, you can click Update Firmware.

Account Details can be seen by clicking on its link. There is an option for Link Cartridges; you can install a cartridge using this window. If you buy a Cricut Access subscription, you can access it through the Cricut Access link.

The setting option is for adjusting keyboard shortcuts, measurements, and turning the grid on and off. The Legal option is to inform you about the policies and Terms of use etc. of the device. The help button is for whenever you are stuck. You can watch helpful videos and read guidelines to help you. Country Select link helps in managing the purchase and setting the correct currency.

The sign-out link is for signing out of your account.

How to Create and Customize a Ready-To-Make Project?

Select a project of your choice, which is in the project tab of the home screen. Once you open the project, its details will be shown. The photo, difficulty level, the time required, materials required, finished size, and instructions are all given.

If you want the project to be the same, then click on the green Make it button. If you want to customize the image, you click customize. You will be taken to Canvas. Once the changes are done, click on the preview. When satisfied, click on the 'Make it an icon.'

How to Start a New Project?

From the home screen, click on the New Project button. You will be directed to an empty Canvas page. You can also access it through Design Space Home Screen by clicking on the new project tile. Editing and adding photos, images, and text are all done here.

You can browse from different projects in the Projects tab. You can browse and insert from Cricut's image library or upload by clicking Images. You can basically shape like circles and squares by the Shape option. You can upload your image by clicking on the Upload option

My project link allows you to open prior projects. The Save option is for saving the current project. When done, cut your project by clicking on the 'Make it an option.'

On the Edit bar, there are many functions to choose from Undo, Redo, select all/deselect, edit which has cut, copy, paste options, align, arrange, flip, size, rotate and position.

On the Text Edit Bar, there are many features. Fonts, when clicked, will display a large variety of their types, and you can browse it by search too. There is also Style, Letter space, Line space, Alignment, and Advance options. The advance option enables you to group different texts.

On the right, there will be a Layers Panel. Image features are given in this area like Contour, Slice, etc. Besides, layers are controlled from here. You can Duplicate, Delete, Group/Ungroup, define line layer, or color.

How to Use the Cricut Image Library?

A most important aspect of Designing is the use of the proper image that you have in mind. Cricut Design Space provides thousands and thousands of beautiful and fresh images to choose from its library. The number grows every day as new images are added. The design space allows the use of the image before purchasing it so that when you purchase it, you don'thave any regrets.

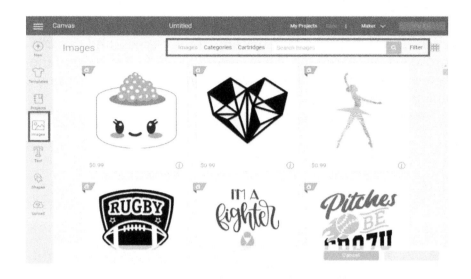

How to Insert the Necessary Images?

First, open the Images which are on the left side of the Canvas in the Design Panel. A new window will pop up, showing all the images in the library and also the uploaded ones.

On top of the screen, three links are showing, Images, Categories, Cartridges. By default, the images will open, showing all the images in the library. You can click on the Categories tab and search in the 50 + categories provided. In the Cartridges tab, in alphabetical order, different cartridges images will be shown. Cartridges are sets of images.

You can also search an image typing the name or tag in the search box, and also filter your search by ownership, layer, and type.

The image information can be seen by clicking the icon lower right corner of the image. Its name, number, cartridge set name (if any), level of access (purchased, owned, free) are all displayed.

The images with intricate designs and have an option for print and cut. There is a printer icon for them in the bottom right of the preview image.

Image Tray is where all of the selected images are temporarily stored for use. When in canvas, click the insert images button to insert the image on the canvas.

The cancel button text you back to the Canvas without any images selected.

Insert images option will insert all the selected images into Canvas

How to Upload an Image?

There are many images to choose from in the library, but it also encourages the use of your images. Images are categorized into two types. The first type of image and the second is the Pattern.

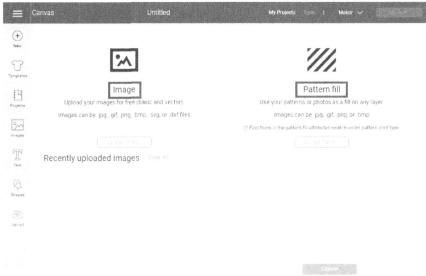

About Images:

Images also have two types, Basic and the other one is Vector. Necessary images like JPG, GIF, PNG, are uploaded as one layer. Uploading the image will require a few steps that the software will guide through. There are two ways to use the image.

First, by print and cut features, print the image and then calibrate the Cricut to cut around it.

Second, is to cut only the outer edges of the image directly on the machine.

Vector files come in SVG Def. files, which are not uploaded as a single layer but multiple layers. Other imported images from different software can also be uploaded. You can search the uploaded image by searching its name/tag. Moreover, all uploaded images can be seen by applying the filter uploaded.

About Patterns:

Uploaded patterns can be seen in the Layers Attributes Panel under the Pattern option. Files that can be uploaded are JPG, PANG, GIF, BMP. When uploading, choose appropriate tags and names for easy searching. You can also access this by clicking uploaded in Patterns filter.

How to Upload an Image from Photoshop?

Cricut Design Space does not allow you to make changes to the images that you want to use. If changes are to be made to the design, then another software like Adobe Photoshop should be used first. Adobe Photoshop does not save vector files, so if the picture has multiple layers, it will be compressed into one. Images best work in jpg. Files, but others can also be used. Firstly, make the required changes in the image using Photoshop. Then save the file in jpg. Format and name, it.

How to Upload an Image from Adobe Illustrator?

Adobe Illustrator is mainly a vector software that can save files in SVG. and Def. formats. It can also save in JPG, and other formats as well. Cricut Design Space can compress the multilayer image into one. In addition to using print and cut, cutting the outline, you can cut different shapes.

- For SVG. Files: After completing the design, click 'Save As' under the File menu. Now name the file and select AutoCAD interchange file.
- For Def. and others: After completing the design, click 'Export,' then 'Export As' under the file menu. Now name the file and select 'AutoCAD interchange file.'

How to Upload an Image from CorelDraw?

CorelDraw is mainly a vector software that can save files in SVG. and Def., formats. It can also save in JPG. and other formats also.

To create vector files, after making suitable changes to the image, select Save As under the File Menu. After giving it a name, select Def.-AutoCAD for SVG-AutoCAD. Accept any default settings if prompted.

To create essential files, after making suitable changes to the image select Export. Then select Export As under the file menu. After giving the name, select JPG, GIF, PNG, or BMP. Use JPG for maximum results. Accept any default settings if prompted.

How to Select an Image?

It is easy to select an image onto the Canvas. There are four methods for this task:

- First, select an image from inside the Canvas. When an image is selected, it will be shown in the Layers Panel in the highlighted form, and a bounding box will appear around the image.
- Either, select an image from the Layers Panel. This will also select the image on your Canvas screen.
- Another option is to select an image from drawing a box. Then draw a box around the image that is entirely inside it. The box will turn blue, and the image will be selected.
- If there is one image, select the 'Select All' option. If there is more than one image, then all of it will be selected.

Working with Uploaded Photos

It is easy to upload your images. There are two methods: First is to upload as images and second by patterns.

Images

- Select the option for upload images under the upload page
- Browse your photo by name and select it.
- If it is a photo, then select the option 'Complex Image' under the upload screen. Then click 'Continue.'

- For the photo to retain its details, it should be used in print and cut. It is done by default, and it is saved as print and cut image. Now click save.
- Back on your upload screen, click on the photo and then click insert. The photo is now ready to use.

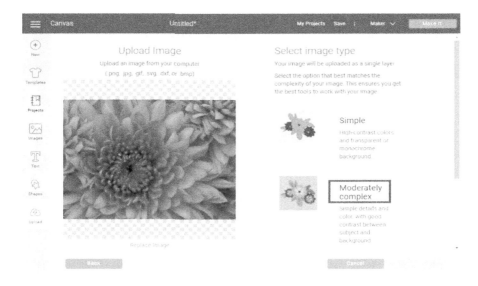

This photo can be manipulated using different tools such as slip tool, or flatten tool. The slip tool can be used to cut the photo or cut images out of the photo. The flatten tool can insert different images on the photo.

Patterns

- Select the option for upload pattern under the upload screen.
- Browse the photo using its name and selected.
- Name and add appropriate tags to your photo to make searching easy.

- Now click Save, a new blue page will pop up telling that the photo is uploaded.

A shape can be used to cut the image to make a pattern. First, insert a shape in the Canvas. Open the 'Layers Attributes Panel' under the 'Image Layers' option. Now select 'Line Types' and then 'Patterns.' Different patterns will open along with the photo. Select the desired photo and fill in the shape. Use different editing tools to your likings, like rotate, scale, pan, and mirror.

Design Space Troubleshooting

Having Some Cricut Design Space-Related Problems?

Is your app crashing, freezing, loading slowly, or not even opening at all?

You are unhappy about the situation because you want to start a new project, right?

These issues are widespread, and as such, we'll explore a few tips on actions to take when you're faced with Design Space problems.

Fixing Cricut Design Space Issues When you put everything into consideration, it is safe to say that the Design Space software is very good.

No system is perfect, and there's always room for improvements, but on the whole, the software works excellently for several projects. However, there are a couple of related issues that are predominant with the software, including; freezing, slow loading, crashing and not opening at all. When you're faced with these issues, there are several things you can do to fix them, including:

Slow Internet Connection

Without saying much, you must understand that a slow internet connection is one of the main causes of Design Space problems. Poor internet connection translates into problems for the software because it requires consistent download and upload speeds to function optimally.

Several websites only require good download speeds e.g. YouTube, thus users on these sites can do away with slow upload speeds. However, unlike those sites, Cricut Design Space requires good upload and download speeds to function optimally because users are constantly sending and receiving information as they progress with their designs.
Note: If you're using a modem, you're likely to have a more stable connection if you move closer to it.

Run a Speed Test

You can use a service like Ookla to run an internet speed test. For Design Space to run optimally, Cricut specifies the following:

- Broadband connection
- Minimum 1 – 2 Mbps Upload
- Minimum 2 – 3 Mbps Download

After running the speed test, if the results are not good, and you are convinced that the connection is affecting your Design space issues, you should wait until the connection improves or you call your service providers.
There is also the option of switching to a new internet service provider with a proper internet connection.

Your Computer

If you run a speed test and realize that your connection is fine, then your computer, mobile phone or tablet might be the problem. Cricut has specific requirements for Design Space to function optimally. Below are some of the requirements:

Windows Computers

Your computer:

- Must have at least 4GB of ram
- Must be running on Windows 8 or later
- Must have Bluetooth connection or a free USB port
- Must have at least 50MB of free disk space
- Must have AMD processor or Intel Core series

Apple Computers

For Design Space to work optimally in your Mac computer, it must have the following:

- At least 50MB free space
- 4GB Ram
- Mac OS X 10.12 or a later version
- CPU of 1.83 GHz

Background Programs

If you're running too many background programs while using Design Space, it might also be a problem.

Some multi-tasking crafters are fond of engaging in different activities while designing on Design Space. For example, some simultaneously chat on Facebook, while downloading movies, watching videos on YouTube, and designing on Design Space. These activities will affect your app and make it malfunction badly, thus it is important to shut down other projects and focus solely on Design Space.

While it is important to close other apps and shut down other activities, there are other things should also do.

Run a Malware Check

If you're using windows, you should upgrade you drivers iii.
   Clear your history and cache

Defragment your Hard Drive

Check your anti-virus software and update if needed. If you execute these tests, it might speed up the system, or even solve all related problems.

Your Browser

Your Design Space software might be having issues due to your system browser.
For you to access Design Space, Cricut recommends that you use the latest version of the browser you use. Be it Edge, Chrome, Firefox or Mozilla; just make sure that it is up to date. If it refuses to work on a particular browser, open it in another browser to see if it works. Although the reasons are unknown, sometimes its works and even works perfectly.

Contact Cricut

If you've tried all possible options and nothing works, you may have to call Cricut customer care to look into the issues you're faced with.

Cricut Cutting Problems and Solutions

Sometimes Cricut machines don't cut correctly and it is a common problem.

For example, you spend hours buying materials and designing your project, but when the machine starts cutting, it destroys your material. This is something that has happened to a lot of people and will keep happening to those that have no idea about it in the future.

With that said, let's explore the possible solutions to the problem.

If you're faced with cutting problems, you have to check the following:

- Is your material sitting flat on your mat?
- Is your mat clean?
- Are you sure you're using the right mat for the material you're cutting?
- Is your blade clean?
- Is your blade dull?
- Are you using the right blade for the material you're cutting?

How to Change Settings?

1. Use the dial to change the cutting settings

2. Use cardstock+ on the dial if you're using heavy cardstock

3. If you're using the custom setting, turn the dial to custom. A list of materials will show up on your computer screen and you'll be able to choose the specific material you intend to cut.

4. Use washi setting if you're using vinyl to cut your small or intricate design.

To do this, you have to turn your dial to custom and look for washi in the prompt that will pop up.

Change the Font and Size

Sometimes, some images are just too intricate or too small to cut. Thus, if your image consists of intricate details or maybe you're using a distinctive font, then it might not cut properly until you get your size sorted.

If possible, you will have to delete some part of your design, increase the size of your image, bolden the font or change/increase the font size. You can use a different program to thicken your font.

Tips to Ensure You Get a Perfect Cut

- Make sure you run a test cut before you go ahead to cut your project
- Ensure that you have the image 'set to cut' and not write or print.
- Make sure to reflect your image and flip the paper over if you are using a piece of shiny cardboard. By doing this, you help the machine cut dull without sticking to the blade and carcass.
- If you're using cardstock, flip over the textured side and make use of the smooth side always.

- If you successfully cut your project with tiny fonts, you can try reverse weeding to make it easier to transfer, especially if you're using vinyl.

The recommendations above are very helpful and will solve most of your cutting problems. However, if you've done everything and nothing seems to work, you should contact Cricut support. They are highly responsive and proactive. We know how most customer care service people behave at times, but with Cricut, you'll be dealing with a world-class team that is set up to help solve product-related issues.
On a final note, if you have explored all your options (including contacting Cricut support), and your cutting problem persists, it is possible that the brand or type of material you're using might be the problem. There are known cases where some brands of vinyl cardstock turned out to be bad for cutting.

CRICUT PROJECT IDEAS

The Best Project Ideas to Make with Your Cricut Machine

The Most Profitable Project Ideas to Make Money with Cricut Even if You're a Newbie

In case you're attempting to extend your innovativeness for utilizing the Cricut Maker, there are numerous tasks that you can take on with unlimited potential outcomes.

There are numerous extraordinary things about the Cricut creator machine that will make you need to utilize it to an ever-increasing extent.

Even though there's a wide assortment of undertakings, utilizing your creative mind for DIY activities will demonstrate that you have an imaginative and one-of-a-kind eyes with regards to using this machine.

Fabric

1. Blankets

The Cricut group has been making propels in bettering its design quality for blanket making.

Cricut has cooperated with Riley Blake Designs to give crafters a wide assortment of sewing designs inside the example library.

You can precisely remove the correct examples for sewing and make the ideal blanket easily.

2. Felt Dolls and Soft Toys

You might need to make toys without anyone else as a DIY. The Cricut producer effectively enables you to cut examples for delicate felt dolls and fragile toys. Aren't these two above unbelievably sweet!?

3. Infant Clothes

The Cricut Maker can slice boards up to 12 X 24. So, while it will be dubious about making grown-ups garments with it, it is extraordinary for making infant dress.
Make and slice designs, so you to make child shirts, onesies, shirts and that's only the tip of the iceberg.

4. Doll Clothes

Since you're going to make dolls with the Cricut Maker, you can make them adorable little doll equips that will make them look increasingly one of a kind.
Make a multicolor doll dress that will make your Cricut dolls stand apart among your locally acquired dolls.

5. Texture Christmas Projects (Ornaments and Christmas Stockings)

Utilizing the Cricut Maker will make cutting texture for making decorations and Christmas leggings a breeze. This machine is ideal for designing unique texture adornments or potentially leggings.
The machine has an example library that you can use to mix various looks of Christmas or occasion improvements.
Primarily utilize the machine to remove your example and after that sew it together.

6. Texture Appliques

Although you'll require a reinforced texture cutting edge in lodging, you can likewise make a progression of texture appliques.

These cutting edges must be bought independently at the same time when you have one. You can make a wide range of complicatedly designed appliques with your applique textures. Critical to take note of that not at all like with the revolving cutting edge, the reinforced texture edge requires you to have strong support on your material.

7. Texture Keyrings

Very easy to make and developing progressively well-known are texture keyrings. There are easy designs in the example library. Dress your keys up with stylish texture keyrings.

8. Texture Coasters

In case you're needing liners for your end tables or some other zone of your home, office or somewhere else, make them with the Cricut Maker.

9. Stick Cushions

It's conceivable you will do a ton of sewing with the Cricut Maker. As you get the majority of your lovely designs cut out, you're going to require a sticky pad to hold every one of your pins.

There are diverse stick pad designs in the example library. As it is, you can get imaginative and make your unique ones as well.

10. Pads and Cushions

Since the machine trims 12 X 24 estimated designs, you can make bunches of various pads and pads for your bed, chairs, lounge chairs, and niches. You can make a few incredible designs to tidy up your home.

Remember that you can remove iron-on vinyl on your producer as well, so why not take your pad design to the following level.

Glass

1. Raised Letters

Make a treat container or a personalized vessel to hold pretty much anything. It would be an extraordinary blessing thought for an educator, mother, father, or companion. Utilize a single word or a platitude to express your affections for the beneficiary. All you need is a compartment, a paste firearm or some raised letter-formed stickers, and some splash paint. Visit the Lettered Cottage to perceive how charming and straightforward this venture is.

2. Carved Drinking Glasses

You don't have to realize how to draw for this task, and you need to brush on some carving dissolvable. Particularly decent is the way that these are washable, not only for looks. Perceive how to make these by visiting A Beautiful Mess.

3. Vintage String Holders

It is an ideal method to shield string balls from getting all hitched up. What's more, they are so adorable! It would seem that they're sucking up a long string of spaghetti. An incredible undertaking for children, as well. Locate the instructional exercise at Handmade Charlotte.

4. Sewn Jar Cover

Shirt yarn is utilized to make these stitched spreads that resemble little sweaters. You can undoubtedly make your shirt yarn using any old or undesirable shirts that you have. The stitch example is found at LVLY. It's an easy task thus charming with the additional lace.

5. Snowman Luminary

This little snowman looks cold with his soft snow finish. Put a battery-worked light inside, and it sparkles! Safe to utilize anyplace in the house or hold tight the tree. Go to Club Chica Circle for the instructional exercise to make this winter light. Keep in mind, and the snowman is proper throughout the entire winter.

6. Pumpkin Jack-o-Lanterns

It is conceivable to think about pumpkin or a jack-o-light as being "exquisite," at that point that is the thing that I'd call this design. In case you're searching for an option in contrast to cutting pumpkins this year, consider this specialty venture for your Halloween party. Locate the instructional exercise at Chica Circle.

7. Sequin-Enhanced Vase

An astonishing expansion to the ordinary Mason container jar: Beautiful sequins makes a downplayed and novel design for a wedding gathering or occasion party. Don't the sequins flicker like little air pockets? Locate the instructional exercise at It All Started with Paint.

8. Cranberry Glass

I think these are so exquisite looking they give any container a makeover suitable for a wedding. You'll discover the headings for this task at homework.

9. Starry Night Luminaries

You'll locate the instructional exercise for making these at Shabby Creek Cottage. They recommend utilizing the lights as wedding embellishments. I figure they would likewise be pleasant, and fitting, for Christmas stylistic layout. It is an extremely straightforward venture that even little youngsters will appreciate.

10. Tissue Decoupage Bottles

Would you like to include a touch of shading without a ton of cost? These tissue paper decoupage jugs will consist of the hues that you need in your stylistic theme with almost no time. You'll locate the instructional exercise at Crafting a Green World. So straightforward and easy, yet a lovely expansion to any room!

11. Hanging Mason jar Light

Okay, accept this is an upcycled old restroom vanity light? If you cherish this, you can locate a utilized vanity light strip at a carport deal, swap meets. Or second-hand shop and make your very own effectively. The directions are found at Remodelaholic.

12. Turkey Jar

In addition to the fact that this is little turkey a social improvement, it can likewise hold confections, or nuts as a cute gift. Locate the instructional exercise at About Family Crafts.

13. Penny Lanterns

Here's an extraordinary thought for utilizing a portion of the pennies you no uncertainty have gathering in a heap someplace since it's a lot of issues conveying them with you. These little lights are appealing. Discover the guidelines at DIY Showoff.

14. Ocean Glass Votive

Make a rich votive by following the instructional exercise given at a Pumpkin and a Princess. A few of these ocean glass votive in various shapes and sizes would be stunning. If you don't have ocean glass, consider utilizing shells.

15. Wind Chimes

You'll locate the instructional exercise at Saved by Love Creations. Any globules may be utilized here, alongside old neckbands or bits of metal.

16. Blessing Purse

It must be so lovely to give a blessing. Think about all the little endowments that would be made significantly increasingly insightful in this sort of wrapping. Discover the guidelines at In My Style.

17. Group Lights

You can consider going to Home Talk for the instructional exercise. It would be an incredible expansion to a yard or patio. I can even envision it utilized as a Christmas adornment by including an occasion shaded strip and greenery.

18. Town Silhouette

It is such a straightforward however excellent thought for a Christmas focal point. It truly makes you incline that you're taking a gander at Christmas' past. Locate the instructional exercise at Shabby Art Boutique.

19. Exquisite Cloche

Change any old compartment into a minor ringer container to grandstand any gathering. Get more instructions on the most proficient method to make a cloche.

20. Container of Fireflies

Make getting fireflies overly easy by amassing this holder of artificial flickering bugs. Shine in obscurity paint, and a few catches give you the appearance of fireflies without the pursuing. Locate the instructional exercise at By Stephanie Lynn.

Tips, Tricks and Shortcuts to Save Your Time and Money

The Cricut Maker and Explore Air 2 are great machines that can be used to do a lot of things. However, new and first-time owners find it a little challenging to get their heads over the machines, making it difficult for them to utilize the machines to their full potentials.

For crafters that get little or no support from experienced users, it takes quite some time for them to really get a hold of the machines and finally maximize their output.

If you've purchased or intend to purchase a Cricut machine, then you must know that there are tips and tricks you can apply to boost the machine's output and ensure optimum functionality.

Most of the tips are geared towards helping beginners understand their Cricut machines; however, there are also other advanced tips for veterans. Below are some of the tips and tricks:

Make Sure You Subscribe to Cricut Access

If you own a Cricut Explore Air 2, you have to subscribe to Cricut Access in order to get the best out of it. There are two subscription plans—the yearly plan and the monthly plan. Having an active subscription plan with Cricut Access will save you a lot of money because you won't have to buy individual projects and images. With Cricut Access, you'll have access to thousands of projects and over 375 fonts. Plus, it's less stressful to pay a flat than to always worry about the amount of money you'll be spending on projects.

Always De-Tack Your Cutting Mat

The Cricut Maker comes with the blue light grip mat, while the Explore Air 2 normally comes with the green standard cutting mat. Before putting the machine, make sure you always place your materials onto the mat first.
When you buy the Explore Air 2, the green mat that comes with it is very sticky. Thus, as a reward for your first project, peel off the plastic cover and place a clean, dry T-shirt over the mat.
Even with the right tools, it can be very difficult to get off the cardstock when it's new, and this results in damaged projects sometimes. The blue light grip mat doesn't have such problems; thus, instead of de-tacking the green mat, you can purchase it for your card and paper projects.

Make Sure You Keep Your Cutting Mat Covers

New cutting mats always come with a plastic shield that covers them, and they are easily pulled off and on. Whatever you do, make sure you don't misplace the cover, and always put it back on the mat whenever you're done using it—this practice helps to keep the mat sticky and clean for over longer periods.

Make Sure You Clean the Cutting Mat

Whenever you use your cutting mat, make sure you clean it afterward, and it is recommended that you use nonalcoholic baby wipes. If you do this consistently, it'll reduce the buildup of vinyl and cardstock residue, as well as dust stains and other regular lint that float about.

Make Sure You Acquire the Right Tools

To fully maximize the Cricut machine experience, you have acquired the Cricut toolset. The set contains a scraper, a weeding tool, a spatula, and scissors. If your craft involves cutting either heat transfer vinyl or adhesive vinyl, then the weeding tool is a must. The other tools come in handy for different activities and projects.

Purchase the Scoring Stylus

The scoring stylus is mandatory for a whole lot of card projects. Thus, without it, your options will be limited, and it doesn't come with the machine at purchase. However, if you buy your machine as part of a bundle, there's a high probability that it'll be included, so you need to check.

Your First Project Should Be Your Sample Project

As a beginner, who just bought the Cricut machine, your first project should be the sample project. When you purchase the Explore Air 2, you'll realize that the machine is loaded with sample cardstock for users to make their first cards. The supporting materials are minimal and it is just one card. Thus, instead of embarking on a huge and fancy project, you can embark on a simple project so that you can get a feel of how things work—hardware and software-wise.

Test Cuts

Before you carry out any serious project, make sure to do a test cut first, because there are a number of things that can possibly go wrong. For example, if you set the blade too high, it might not cut the cardstock or vinyl properly. Also, if you set the blade too low, it could possibly ruin the cutting mat. Executing a test cut involves checking the settings of the machine and asking the machine to cut a small circle, maybe.

Make Sure You Always Replace Pen Lids after Use

A lot of crafters have the habit of forgetting their pen inside the machine when they're done with their projects. It can happen to anyone but make sure the pen ink doesn't dry out; it is important to get the lid on it as soon as you're done with your project. The Cricut pen is very expensive, and maybe that's the reason why Design Space always prompts users to get their lids back on.

You Should Link Your Old Cartridges to Your Design Space Account

If you have any Cricut cartridges from a previous Cricut machine; you can link them up to your new account. The procedure is fast and simple; however, you have to understand that each cartridge can only be linked once. Thus, if you intend to buy a used cartridge, you have to confirm that it hasn't been linked to another account already.

Getting Materials off the Cutting Mat

Rather than using conventional tools for removing vinyl or cardstock from the cutting mat, you can consider another method. When people peel their projects from the mat, it can possibly result in curling; thus, you should peel the mat away from the project instead. In addition, you should also do the unconventional method of bending the mat away from the card.

When you do this, the mat might turn upside down and bend one corner to leave the cardstock. At this stage, you can just place the spatula under to take off your project. Some people use their credit cards to take off the mat, and as much as this might work, it can also damage the adhesive on the mat.

Purchase the Deep Cut Blade

One of the most painful things in the world of crafting is embarking on a project without the right tools. Unlike the Maker, you need to have the deep cut blade for the Explore Air 2 to be able to cut through thicker leather, card, chipboard, and others. When you order the blade, you should also order the blade housing too. Furthermore, you don't have to wait till you need it urgently before you order it. Buy it today.

Use Free SVG Files in Order to Cut the Cost

In terms of designing projects, you don't have to be fully dependent on the Design Space store. You have other options; there's the option of creating your personal SVG files or using some other free SVG files on the internet. There are a number of websites on the internet that have so many free SVG files. All you have to do in order to locate them is to carry out minimal research on the internet.

Make Sure You Load the Mat Properly

Before you start cutting, you must be sure that your mat is loaded properly. It must be placed under the rollers. If the mat is not loaded properly, the machine may not cut at all, or in other cases, it might start cutting before the top of the grip on the mat.

Different Pens Work in the Explore Air 2

The Cricut pens are not the only ones that work in the Explore Air 2 machine. Examples of other pens that can work with the machine include, but are not limited to, American Craft Pens and Sharpie Pens. With that said, you should have it at the back of your mind that Cricut pens are of the highest quality and are known to last longer than others.

Make Use of Free Front for Some of Your Projects

On the internet, there are a number of websites where you can get free fonts to use for your designs. To do this, you need to visit the sites and download the fonts, install them to your system and load them on your Cricut Design Space.

Installation of Fonts into Design Space

When you install the fonts, the next step is to load them into Design Space. Thus, in order to achieve this, you have to sign out of Design Space and re-sign in. After that, you'll also have to restart your PC. When this is done, you can check your Design Space account, where you'll see the new fonts in the display.

Changing/Replacing Blades

Just like everything in life, nothing lasts forever, and Cricut blades are known to wear out. You will know it's time to change the blade when the cuts are no longer effective and smooth. That is the most obvious sign; however, there are others, including:

- Tearing vinyl or card

- Lifting of vinyl off the backing sheet

- Halfway cuts (wrong cut settings can also be responsible for this).

If you're convinced that your blades are no longer effective, you have to purchase new ones.

When the Mat Is No Longer Sticky

The most proactive way of keeping your mat healthy over a long period is by cleaning it. However, if the mat is beyond redemption and there is no replacement yet, you should tape down your vinyl or card for it to stick. While tapping, you shouldn't tape the areas that are meant to be cut; just tape the sides. Most people use the medium-tack painter tape because it allows a lot of room for this type of action, and it does not damage the cardstock.

Custom Settings for Cricut Machines

There are 7 preset options on the dial for Explore Air 2, and they include:

1. Cardstock
2. Paper
3. Iron-on
4. Vinyl
5. Poster board
6. Light cardstock
7. Bonded fabric

There is a custom option for materials that are not included in the cutting list, and you select it on the dial.
To do this, open Design Space, choose your project, and press 'Make it.' At this point, you'll see a prompt with a drop-down menu, where you'll be able to choose your material.
Likewise, you can also create a new custom material. There are resources on the Cricut website and all over the internet regarding the creation of custom material.

Use the Right Blade for the Right Material

There are a number of crafters out there that use separate blades for cutting each material, e.g., let's say a crafter uses a dedicated blade to cut vinyl and another dedicated blade to cut cardstock. This practice is important because, from experience, different materials wear blades differently. Thus, it is easier for the blade to cut vinyl than to cut through the card. If you have a particular blade for cutting vinyl materials, it means that the blade will be in prime condition. However, if you have a common blade that cuts everything, it'll easily go blunt and begin to find it difficult to cut through vinyl.

Whenever You Cut HTV, Always Mirror Your Image

Make sure you mirror your design if you're cutting heat transfer vinyl with a Cricut machine. Whenever you hit the 'Make It' button, there is always an option for you to mirror your design. Thus, it is recommended that you use this option for each mat.

Make Sure Your HTV Is Properly Placed on the Cutting Mat

If you intend to cut heat transfer vinyl, you have to place the shiny side of the vinyl down on the cutting mat. The whole idea is for the carrier sheet to be down and the dull side on top. This can be a little bit confusing at times, but you have to remember this: shiny side down always.

For Small and Intricate Designs, Use Weeding

Weeding boxes are important, especially if you are cutting out a number of designs on a sheet of vinyl or just cutting out a little intricate design.
In Cricut Design Space, use the square tool to add a box around your design and join both elements together.
Manipulate it into a rectangle by unlocking the shape at the bottom left corner.
When you do this, you'll realize that it is easier than concurrently weeding different designs on a sheet of vinyl. It is also easier than looking for your designs and using scissors to cut them out separately.

Always Set the Dial

This is one of the best tips ever, but crafters tend always to forget to change the material settings on the machine. It is funny because before cutting, Cricut Design Space tells crafters the type of materials the dial is set to; however, it is not uncommon for them to overlook it and proceed to cut. Most times, crafters get overexcited after designing, which they only have cut in their minds.
Mind you, setting your dial can save you the mistake of not cutting through your cardstock or cutting right through your cutting mat—the choice is yours.

Always Have a Constant Supply of Materials

Just like it was said earlier, it is very hurtful to execute a project without the proper tools, e.g., I have been in the position of lacking the right pen for a project, being without the scoring stylus, not having a deep cut blade, etc. Furthermore, just imagine that you are about to start a project, and you suddenly realize that you don't have cardstock, HTV, or adhesive vinyl—it can be pretty sad.

Thus, you should always have a healthy supply of materials at all times, including: Cricut adhesive vinyl, a pad containing different colors of cardstock, and Cricut iron-on vinyl or a color bundle of Siser Easy Weed HTV.

If you have these items on hand, it is highly unlikely that you'll be caught out before or during the execution of any project.

Bonus: Project Ideas for Birthday, Cake Design and for All Seasons

Gift box

For this DIY project, you just need to cut a sheet of cardstock on your Cricut machine using a pretty filigree design. Then just fold it, glue or tape it and add a ribbon to keep it closed. Now just pop in an LED tea light into it and watch it light up. This is a super easy project with a big creative factor.

Materials for this DIY project:

1. 80 lb. or 105 lb. 12" x 12" cardstock for the boxes

2. Pretty ribbon to keep the top of the treat box closed

3. Tacky glue and tape

4. LED tealights (optional)

Cupcake Wrappers

This is a great project to do with the children or just for a themed party. It will help to set just the right image for your guests!

You'll need:

- Paper or card

That's it!

Procedures:

Step 1

Take a look at the Design Space site and select the design or designs that appeal to you the most. The great thing about these designs is that you can create more than you need and save the extra for another occasion.

Your image will need to be approximately 9 inches long to wrap around a standard cupcake.

Step 2

Load your card in the machine and send the image or images. Within a few minutes, they should all be printed and cut.

Step 3

Wrap the card around your cupcake and clip it together by making a small incision in each end. If you've used an actual cupcake design from Design Space the tab will already be present.
An alternative is to overlap the end and use a dot of glue to hold the two ends together.
Top Tip: When doing a children's party, you can actually create the designs and get the children to decorate them before you wrap them around the cupcakes.

Pie Stencil

Project thanks to Cricut Design Space

Another holiday project can come in the form of a sweet treat using this stencil for the powdered sugar. If you want a smaller idea, adapt this same concept to fit the inside of a coffee mug. Sprinkle cinnamon or another spice over the top of your latte for a lovely morning pick-me-up.
For this project, you need cardstock and a weeding tool, in addition to your pie and powdered sugar.

Procedures:

Step 1

Write your message in Design Space. Make sure to adjust your font size and layout to fit the dimensions of your pie.

Step 2

Cut out your words from the cardstock and weed out the center of any letters you do not want to be part of the design.

Step 3

Place the cardstock over your pie. Consider placing a piece of wax paper around the edges of your pie to rest the stencils so the paper does not rest on the pie directly.

Step 4

Using a sifter, sift the powdered sugar over the top of the stencil. When finished, gently and carefully lift the stencil off the pie to reveal the message. Remove the wax paper and throw it away. Serve the pie as soon as possible after using the sugar to minimize any changes to the sugary message.

Leftover Boxes

Send your guests off in style with these adorable leftover boxes. This two-step project combines customized stickers and sweet little boxes. If you want to, skip the boxes and attach the stickers to store-bought bags or other containers. Or go wild and offer guests a combination of to-go containers to choose from!

Pick up a few pages of sticker paper and cardstock that is corrugated cardboard. Look for interesting patterns or keep it simple, if you prefer. The cardboard will be used for the bottom of your to-go boxes. Purchase coordinating traditional cardstock to make the lid to the boxes. Additionally, you will need glue or glue tape to adhere to the edges of the box together. If you are offering guests a variety of to-go options, like bags or other, store-bought boxes, make sure to pick some of those up as well for your stickers.

Procedures:

Step 1

Design your sticker template. Include a nice border from the Design Space Library, and text indicating when the leftovers were from to help guests keep track of how long they have had the leftovers. Adjust the size of your stickers to fit the to-go boxes, about 1.75" X 1.5", and to attach to other bags or boxes, about 5' X 4".

Step 2

Print your stickers and then cut them apart using your Cricut.

Step 3

In Design Space Library, search for the pie box template. It is free and easy to load! Print and cut your boxes; load the cardboard for the bottom of the boxes and the traditional cardstock for the top.

Step 4

Part of the cut file from Design Space is instruction for the machine to score your boxes to make assembly easier. Fold along the scored lines and use your glue to attach the edges together. Assemble the tops and bottoms with the same method.

Step 5

Add a sticker to the top of your boxes. If you are using other containers or bags, attach your stickers to them as well.

Felt Roses

Materials needed:

1. SVG files with 3D flower design

2. Felt Sheets

3. Fabric Grip Mat

4. Glue Gun

Procedures:

1. First of all, upload your Flower SVG Graphics into the Cricut design space as explained in the "Tips" section ("How to import images into Cricut Design Space").

2. Having placed the image in the project, select it, right-click and click "Ungroup." This allows you to resize each flower independently of the others. Since you are using felt, it is

recommended that each of the flowers be at least 6 inches in size.

3. Create several copies of the flowers, as many as you wish, selecting the colors you want in the Color Sync Panel (by dragging and dropping the images onto the color you would want them to be cut on). Immediately you're through with that, click on "Make it" on the Cricut design space.

4. Click on "Continue." After your Cricut Maker is connected and registered, under the "materials" options, select "Felt."

5. If your rotary blade is not in the machine, insert it. Next, on the Fabric Grip Mat, place the first felt sheet (in order of color), then, load them into your Cricut Maker. Press the "cut" button when this is done.

6. After they are cut, begin to roll the cut flowers one by one. Do this from the outside in. Make sure that you do not roll them too tight. Use the picture as a guide.

7. Apply Hot Glue on the circle right in the middle and press the felt flowers that you rolled up on the glue. Hold this in place and do not let it go until the glue binds it.

8. Wait for the glue to dry, and your roses are ready for use.

Hand Lettered Cake Topper

Materials needed:

1. Glitter Card Stock

2. Gold Paper Straw

3. Cutting Mat

4. Hot Glue Gun

Procedures:

1. Create your design in Cricut Design Space, or download your desired design and import it into Cricut Design Space using the instructions in the "Tips" section.

2. Resize the design as required.

3. Click the "Make it" button.

4. Select Glitter card stock as your material in Design Space and set the dial on your Cricut machine to "Custom."

5. Place the glitter card stock on your Cutting Mat and load it into the Cricut machine.

6. When this is done, press the "Cut" button on your Cricut machine.

7. After the machine is done with cutting the design, remove it from the mat. This can be done much more quickly using the Cricut Spatula tool.

8. Finally, using hot glue, stick cut-out design to the Gold Paper Straw and stick it in the cake as shown in the picture.

MAKE MONEY WITH CRICUT

The Ultimate Guide to Master the Art
of Making Money with Cricut

How to Monetize Cricut

Before you start trying to make money from your Cricut, take some time to think about whether or not it really is what you want to do. When I bought Cricut, I thought about starting a personalization and stationery business, but everything in life is trial and error, I am still in the testing phase.
Here are some things to think about before "launching":

- Are you doing it just because your friends say your creations are amazing?
- Do you want to support your family financially?
- Are you doing it for some extra money?
- Are you willing to deal with hard customers? (there are always difficult clients)
- Do you want to turn your hobby into a job?
- Can you learn more about marketing on and off the network?
- Do you have enough time and space to start a small business?
- Do you like to make crafts with your Cricut? So much to do over and over again?

I definitely don't want to discourage you from starting to make money from your Cricut, but you have to put your feet on the ground and I also want you to be smart about it. Your answers to these questions do not necessarily determine your decision whether to launch or not, BUT they will help you realize what it will be like for you to start a small business with your Cricut.

All About Copyright

Since you decided to get into this business, we should talk about licenses and copyrights, as this is the area where you can get into trouble the fastest. And the question why ?, because all the images, cut files that you download or even copies from the Internet were created by someone, and the simple fact of finding them on Google does not give you the right to reproduce it or worse, sell it on the Internet.
There are different policies that protect images; below I describe the most common.

Cricut Angel Policy

Within the same Cricut Design Space system, there is a library of Cricut images to create with the machine. You can create and sell with such designs but under the "Cricut Angel" Policy. Please read this policy carefully, you will find many things there. Some things it mentions:

- Most Cricut Access images are included in this policy.

- Create up to 10,000 items to sell using Cricut images.

- Don't just sell individual images.

- You must include a copyright notice with your projects.

- Do not include licensed content, such as images from Disney or Marvel.

Personal Use vs. Commercial Use

If you prefer to use very specific images, you can buy them in online stores. Don't just download them from Google images and put them in your projects... It is very likely that if you do, you are violating copyrights.

When purchasing images online, be sure to read the file's terms of use. Most of these images only include a personal use license, that is, you cannot create products to sell with these types of files. There may also be the option to buy the same image but with a commercial license, just remember to read the terms.

There are images of licensed characters that normally belong to Disney and/or Marvel, such as (and this will surprise you as much as I do): Elsa from Frozen or Iron Man from Marvel. Using these images is breaking copyright and you may have trouble using them as a way to make money. My advice would be to stay away from using these images, it can bring you an ugly problem and even a lawsuit or fine.

Starting a Cricut Craft Business

Now that we are clear on the Legal topic, let's talk about how to earn money and get the best out of your Cricut.

Define Your Niche

One of the worst things you can do is do whatever people ask you to do. A glass here, a personalization over there, a cake topper from today to tomorrow. You'll end up with lower margins than the market, perhaps wasted product and a confused audience.

I recommend defining your niche and type of product to one or very few elements and/or themes so that you can have a strong and your audience can remember you faster. When deciding what type of products to sell, consider "added value." This can be additional things to your product or just perfect it. In this way, you could charge a "premium" price.

Buy Materials in Large Quantities

Having decided on your niche, you can buy your supplies and materials, what I call "wholesale." This is nothing more than buying large quantities, say 10-foot vinyl rolls, boxes of 10 glasses or cups at cheaper prices than if you buy them per unit. Cricut also sells wholesale materials.

Quality Really Matters

One of the fastest ways to destroy your business is to produce a low-quality product. Word of mouth travels faster than we think, and the worst part is that you can't change the ratings you get if you're selling your product in an online store. Therefore, when you are creating your business, make sure you can consistently produce quality products. If you understand that your quality is falling because you are not in control because you receive many requests, consider seeking help or stopping your orders for a short time.
Whatever you do, do it well.

How to Set the price

It bothers me to see people selling their beautiful super elaborate creations at SO cheap prices. Those people are not even valuing their own time. They are not taking into account your talent, materials or many other things that are important when setting prices.

Monetizing Your Art

You have practiced, perfected, and established a style of that art that you like to do so much. You have decorated cards, personalized objects, created pictures with motivational phrases; and with pride, you have shared your work on social networks.

Now comes the question that scares you so much. "What would you charge to do THIS?" It is super exciting and flattering to know that there are people who ask you to do what you love to earn money.

However, as exciting as it is, it scares us, and a lot. To be honest I still feel nervous when sending a quote to my clients. We have all been there on several occasions, and I know it is difficult at first, but the most important thing is to have everything in order.

Before you start thinking about monetizing your art, you should realize all the factors that you may not have considered when valuing your work. Believe it or not, there are many more reasons behind the prices, apart from "because that is what so-and-so charges." All right then let's get started.

Someone Wants to Hire Me... What Do I Do Now?

Congratulations! You must be super excited, but before responding with a price, or worse, offering to do it for free, there is a lot to consider when evaluating your work, and I hope I'm covering a large part here.

Why is pricing so important? Shouldn't I feel good just by putting the price that I understand "correct?" Well, it is not wrong to ask yourself this question, however, you must be sure that you are not bothering yourself, the client and other artists in the business.

When you are self-employed, you are in charge of the money you earn, so you want to do it right. It is important that you ask yourself these questions before setting a price:

- How much are your time and energy worth to you?

- How does your experience compare to others in the business?
- What are your material costs?
- What is the size of the project?
- What is the project deadline?
- Are you going to include shipping, or charge extra?
- Is this piece going to be original, or is the customer making and selling multiple copies?
- Does the client want you to convert the artwork into a digital format?
- Will you be creating the artwork in your own studio or on-site?
- What will be your minimum charge for small jobs?

Your Time + Energy

This is where the wellness factor comes in, where you need to think about how much your time is worth to you. It's worth a lot more than buying the cheapest combo at McDonald's, but there the questions come... Karissa, how much exactly? How do I find out? It is difficult to answer frankly but there are certain guidelines that I can tell you that can help you.

The typical answer is that you put yourself a monthly salary with which you feel comfortable, I will speak in an imaginary way based on some local statistics of the Dominican Republic to speak with numbers and you can understand. Let's say (I made it up) that on average a monthly salary in my country is $ 15,000 Dominican pesos and this is the number with which you value your time and energy.

This number will be divided by 4.3, this number is established as the average of weeks in the year since there are months that have 30 days, another 31 and February with 28. Already starting to see the difference? Now try to use that math to calculate your own hourly rate.

Start with the monthly salary you feel comfortable with:
_____

Divide that number by 4.3 and put it here:
_____

Now divide this other number by 44 (remember that this number may vary). So this result is your hourly rate that you will put here: _____

Your Level of Experience

You may have been practicing or creating for a week or a year before being asked about working for money. This is more about the quality of your work, rather than how long you've been at it.

NOTE: It is not that you are going to compare with artists who have a level of professionalism for a long time, it is a matter of an objective perspective.

Is it clean? Is consistent? Do you have your own style? Do you feel confident in your work? Have you taken workshops or courses to ensure your techniques are correct?

Cost of Materials

Are you using cheap store markers or artist quality paints? Do you use expensive papers and prepared inks? Are they special items you need? Do you have to order online that are specific to some part of the world or available near you?

The value increases with the quality of your tools and materials, as well as your knowledge of them. If you answer "What kind of paint do you have/do you use?" With an "I don't know... I've had it for a long time and the label it has is no longer visible" or "A friend gave it to me and I don't know where it got it" your work will not be as valuable as that of someone whose answer is "I use Winsor and Newton's lightweight, water-resistant watercolors."

Artist-quality materials cost more, so it's important that you know the cost of your materials in case they run out.

Also, for a big job, you may have to burn seven special markers. That is a part of the cost that you do not want out of your time or pocket but is an expense that must be included in your estimate.

Of course, if in a job you used only part of the material, obviously you are not going to charge the full cost of that material, there you must use mathematics, knowing in advance how much of the material you used and obtaining a percentage.

Project Size

This is probably one of the first factors to value your project. How big is it? Creating something, for example, a lettering composition. It is an 8 ½ x 11-inch sheet with ten words that will take much less time and fewer materials than those same ten words on an 8x10 footboard. You can have a price for measurements, let's say square inches or better use your hourly rate that we work above.

Delivery/Shipping

You must indicate in your budget if the delivery is included or is an extraordinary payment. That means you need to know where the piece is going. You may have to purchase parcel shipping quotes outside of your city based on the weight size and service you really need. I recommend that you investigate the rates of the shipping companies and thus have a standard shipping cost.

Original or continuous use?

Will your client use your art once (like a wedding card), continuously (like a business card or blog), or multiple times (like a T-shirt to resell)? It is always a good idea to ask this question in advance. The answer will help you determine how valuable your artwork is to the customer. If it will be used continuously to promote or generate direct income for your client, the value increases.

Deliverables

What should you deliver to your customer as a finished product? An original art? Or is it digital? Both of them? What file formats? JPG, PNG, TIF, EPS, AI? Do you have experience digitizing, and do you have the best tools to do it?
Spending time digitizing and preparing multiple files takes time and experience, and therefore should be priced accordingly. There are also those printed from digital art. Will you mail the file? In a memory? Digital start and then you delivered it printed? All this must be taken into account considering the time and effort it took to do it.
NOTE: a digital job is even more expensive since it can be reproduced and using specialized programs requires previous experience and learning, which I suppose also costs you to acquire.

Location (In or Out of Your Studio)

Your hourly rate will also largely depend on where you will be doing the work.

When you have the luxury of your own space you can perform several tasks at the same time, that is, you can be working on two projects at the same time. This makes it easy to access all of your supplies and materials. The most convenient way for you to work in your own place, at your own pace with everything you need at hand, you should not worry about traffic.

If the job requires you to be somewhere outside your study (let's say a restaurant for example), the value of your time will increase significantly. You will have to travel to and from the place (which needs to be included in your work time), carry all your materials with you and only commit to that work during the assigned hours. That also means that you will be in an uncontrolled environment, this includes distractions, noise and curious people. It can be a lot of fun working on site, and it can be a real headache.

Sometimes a combination of time in your studio and on-site works best. You can carry out all the designs and preparatory work in the studio so that you are ready to carry out your duties once you arrive on site. This would be shown as two separate hourly rates in the quote, breaking down your activities, so your client knows how they are investing their money in you.

Project Term

Only you know what time is most comfortable for you to work. If not, I recommend measuring the time you take doing your work to have an estimate and also a space in case something unforeseen occurs. If a client comes out of nowhere with a crazy panic because they are the most important in the world, ALWAYS add a fee for speed, clarifying the time it takes you in normal time for similar works, and that you will make an exception for him/her. Normally these prices vary between 50% or 100% of the labor price.

It is best to avoid these types of jobs because you start to get used to the client, only accept these cases if it is strictly necessary.

Your Minimum Price

You have heard the expression "I am not going to get out of bed for less than 1,000 pesos per hour." That is what we have to calculate. What hourly rate makes the project worth your time, energy and experience, in addition to cover any expenses or wear and tear on your supplies?

If someone asks you to do a tiny job, like "write my name," you need to be prepared with your minimum load. Sure, you will not charge her a price per name on an invitation (say $ 50) and she would leave it like that.

Taking into account the time it will take to contact so-and-so for details (style, color, size, delivery, etc.), the time required to assemble your materials and to prepare your workspace (remove the dishes from the dining room table by example, and send or deliver the final piece, $ 50 is not close to cover your time, energy and materials.

If all this advice were useful to you to monetize Cricut, please leave a review about this book!

Why So Many People Get Stuck With Cricut and How to Fix It

Material Tearing or Not Cutting Completely Through

This is the biggest problem with most Cricut users. When this happens, the image is ruined, and you've wasted material. More machines have been returned or boxed up and put away due to this problem than any other.

But don't panic, if your paper is not cutting correctly there are several steps you can take to try and correct the problem. The most important considerations are:

- Anytime you work with the blade, turn your machine off. I know it's easy to forget this because you're frustrated and you're trying this and that to make it work correctly. But this is an important safety precaution that you should remember.

- Make simple adjustments at first. Turn the pressure down one. Did it help? If not, turn the blade down one number. Also, make sure the mat is free of debris so the blade rides smoothly. Usually the thicker the material, the higher the pressure number should be set to cut through the paper. Don't forget to use the multi-cut function if you have that option. It may take a little longer to cut 2, 3, or 4 times, but by then it should cut clean through. For those of you using the smaller bugs that do not have that option here is how to make your own multi-cut function. After the image has been cut, don't unload the mat just hit load paper, repeat last, and cut. You can repeat this sequence 2, 3, or 4 times to ensure your image is completely cut out.

- If you are using thinner paper and it is tearing, try reducing the pressure and slowing down the speed. When cutting intricate designs, you have to give the blade enough time to maneuver through the design. By slowing it down it will be able to make cleaner cuts.
- Clean the edge of the blade to be sure no fuzz, glue, or scraps of paper are stuck to it.
- Make sure the blade is installed correctly. Take it out and put it back so it's seated firmly. The blade should be steady while it's making cuts. If it makes a shaky movement it's either not installed correctly, or there's a problem with the blade housing.
- Be aware that there is a deep-cutting blade for thicker material. You'll want to switch to this blade when you're cutting heavy card stock. This will also save wear and tear on your regular blade. Cutting a lot of thick material will obviously wear your blade out quicker than thinner material and cause you to change it more often.

Machine Freezing

Remember always to turn your machine off when you switch cartridges. When you switch cartridges leaving the machine on it's called "hot-swapping" and it can sometimes cause the machine to freeze. This is more of an issue with the older models and doesn't seem to apply to the Expression 2.

You know how quirky electronic gadgets can be, so give your machine rest for five or ten minutes every hour. If you work for several hours continuously, your machine might overheat and freeze up.

Turn the machine off and take a break. Restart it when you come back and it should be fine. Then remember not to rush programming the machine and give it an occasional rest.

Don't press a long list of commands quickly. If you give it too much information too quickly it will get confused in the same way a computer sometimes does and simply freeze up. Instead of typing in one long phrase try dividing up your words into several cuts.

If you're using special feature keys, make sure you press them first before selecting the letters.

Power Problems

If you turn your machine on and nothing happens the power adapter may be at fault. Jiggle the power cord at the outlet and where it connects to the machine to make sure it's firmly connected. Ideally, you want to test the adapter before buying a new one. Swap cords with a friend and see if that fixed the problem. Replacement adapters can be found on eBay by searching for Cricut adapter power supply.

The connection points inside the machine may also pose a problem; here is how to test that. Hold down the plug where it inserts into the back of the machine and turn it on. If it powers up, then the problem is inside the machine and the connection points will have to be soldered again.

If the machine powers up but will not cut, then try a hard reset. See the resource section for step-by-step instructions on resetting your machine.

Here are a few tips especially for Cricut Expression 2users. Have you turned on your machine, you watch it light up and hear it gearing up but when you try to cut nothing happens? Or you're stuck on the welcome screen or the LCD screen is unresponsive.

Well here are two quick fixes to try. First, try a hard reset sometimes called the "Rainbow Screen Reset" to recalibrate your die cutter. If that does not resolve the problem you're going to have to restore the settings.

To help cut down on errors try to keep your machine updated. When an update is available, you should receive a message encouraging you to install the latest version.

For those of you using third-party software that is no longer compatible with the Cricut you probably already know that updating your machine may disable that software.

When you cut heavy paper and your Cricut Expression 2 shuts down try switching to the normal paper setting and use the multi-cut function.

Carriage Will Not Move

If the carriage assembly does not move, check to see if the belt has broken or if the car has fallen off the track. Provo Craft does not sell replacement parts, which is nuts, so try to find a compatible belt at a vacuum repair shop.

If the wheels have fallen off the track, remove the plastic cover, and look for a tiny screw by the wheel unscrew it. You now should be able to move the wheel back on track.

Unresponsive Keyboard

If you are sure you are pressing the keys firmly, you have a cartridge inserted correctly, and a mat loaded ready to go, but the keypad is still not accepting your selection, the problem may be internal.

You will have to remove the keyboard and check if the display cable is connected to the keypad and to the motherboard. If the connections are secure then you have a circuit board problem, and repairs are beyond the scope of this book.

An important reminder, please do not attempt any repairs unless your machine is out of warranty.

Weird LCD Screen

The LCD screen is now showing strange symbols or is blank after doing a firmware update. Try running the update again making sure your selections are correct.

When the image you choose is bigger than the mat or paper size you selected the preview screen will look grayed out instead of showing the image. So, increase the paper and mat size or decrease the size of your image.

Also, watch out for the gray box effect when using the center point feature. Move the start position down until you see the image appear. The same thing may happen when using the fit to length feature. Try changing to landscape mode and shorten the length size until the image appears.

Occasionally using the "Undo" button will cause the preview screen to turn black; unfortunately, the only thing to do is turn the machine off. Your work will be lost and you have to start again.

Cartridge Errors

Sometimes dust or debris accumulates in the cartridge port, gently blow out any paper fiber that may have collected in the opening. Make sure the contact points are clean and that nothing is preventing the cartridge from being read properly. With any electrical machine overheating can be a problem. If you get a cartridge error after using your machine for a while turn it off and let it cool down for about fifteen minutes.

If this is the very first time you're using the cartridge and you get an error, I'm sure you know the trick about turning the cartridge around and inserting it backward.

If you thought you could use your Imagine cartridges with your Cricut Expression 2, think again. You will get an error message because you can only use the art cartridges that you can cut with, the color and pattern cartridges are for printing. Even brand-new items fresh out of the box can be defective. If you see a cartridge error 1, 2, 3, 4, 5, 6, 9, or 99 call customer service and tell them the name, serial number, and error message number and they may replace the cartridge.

Trouble Connecting to Your Computer

All Cricut machines come with a USB cord that lets you connect to your computer and allows you to use the other products like the Cricut Design Studio software, Cricut Craft Room, or the Cricut Gypsy with your machines.

Double-check your USB connection and try another port. Check to see if you may have a firewall or antivirus software that is blocking the connection.

See if you're running the latest firmware. You may need to update. Older machines update via firmware (Personal Cutter, Expression, Create, and Cake) the newer (Expression 2, Imagine, and Gypsy) use the Sync program to update.

When Anything Else Fails

I know that no one wants to hear this. But there are going to be times when you may have to resort to calling customer service. This is especially true if your machine is still under warranty. You don't want to do anything that might void the warranty on a machine that is truly defective.

Sadly, Prove Craft is known for its long wait times and sometimes less than stellar service. Stick it out and demand that your machine is fixed or replaced.

After a while, you may notice some of your projects coming out in a condition that is less-than-crisp.

Ensure your Machine Is on Stable Footing

This may seem pretty basic but ensuring that your machine is on a level surface will allow it to make more precise cuts every single time. The rocking of the machine or wobbling could cause unstable results in your projects.

Ensure no debris has gotten stuck under the feet of your machine that could cause instability before proceeding to the next troubleshooting step!

Redo All Cable Connections

So, your connections are in the best possible working order, undo all your cable connections, blow into the ports or use canned air, and then securely plug everything back into the right ports. This will help to make sure all the connections are talking to each other where they should be!

Completely Dust and Clean Your Machine

Your little Cricut works hard for you! Return the favor by making sure you're not allowing gunk, dust, grime, or debris to build up in the surfaces and crevices. Adhesive can build up on the machine around the mat input and on the rollers, so be sure to focus on those areas!

Check Your Blade Housing

Sometimes debris and leavings from your materials can build up inside the housings for your blades! Open them up and clear any built-up materials that could be impeding swiveling or motion.

Sharpen Your Blades
A very popular Cricut trick in use is to stick a clean, fresh piece of foil to your Cricut mat, and run it through with the blade you use to sharpen. Running the blades through the thin metal helps to revitalize their edges and give them a little extra staying power until it's time to buy replacements.
Another way to do this is to make a ball of foil, remove the blades from the housing, and stick them into the ball of foil several times until you notice a shine on the blade. This can give you a better idea of how sharpened your blades are becoming before you finish up with them, and it seems like a more expedient way to sharpen several blades in one sitting, but the reviews seem to be equally as positive as letting your machine do the work for you on one blade at a time.

How to Start Selling Your Projects

It is a well-known fact in the world of business that to make money, you first need to invest money. With that being said, if you already own a Cricut cutting machine, then you can jump to the next paragraph, but if you are debating if it's worth the investment, then read on. As mentioned earlier, Cricut has a range of cutting machines with distinctive capabilities offered at a varying price range. The Cricut Explore Air 2 is priced at $249.99, and the Cricut Maker is priced at $399.99 (the older Cricut Explore Air model may be available for sale on Amazon at a lower price). Now, if you were to buy any of these machines during a holiday sale with a bundle deal that comes with a variety of tools, accessories, and materials for a practice project as well as free trial membership to Cricut Access, you would already be saving enough to justify the purchase for your personal usage. The cherry on top would be if you can use this investment to make more money. You can always get additional supplies in a bundle deal or from your local stores at a much lower price. All in all, those upfront costs can easily be justified with the expenses you budget for school projects that require you to cut letters and shapes, create personalized gifts for your loved ones, decorate your home with customized decals, and of course, your own jewelry creations. These are only a handful of the reasons to buy a Cricut machine for your personal use. Let's start scraping the mountain of Cricut-created wealth to help you get rich while enjoying your work! At this stage, let's assume that you have bought a Cricut cutting machine and have enough practice with beginner-friendly projects. You now have the skillset and the tools to start making money with your Cricut machine, so let's jump into how you can make it happen. The ways listed below have been tried and tested as successful money-making strategies that you can implement with no hesitations.

Selling Pre-Cut Customized Vinyl

Vinyl is super beginner-friendly material to work with and comes in a variety of colors and patterns to add to its great reputation. You can create customized labels for glass containers and canisters to help anyone looking to organize their pantry. Explore the online trends and adjust the labels. Once you have your labels designed, the easiest approach is to set up an "Etsy" shop, which is free and very easy to use. It's almost like opening an Amazon prime membership account. If your design is in demand, you will have people ordering even with no advertising. But if you would like to keep the tempo high, then advertise your Etsy listing on Pinterest and other social media platforms. This is a sure-shot way to generate more traffic to your Etsy shop and to turn potential customers into paying customers. An important note here is the pictures being used on your listing. You cannot use any of the stock images from the Design Space application and must use your own pictures that match the product you are selling.

Create a package of 5 or 6 different labels like sugar, salt, rice, oats, beans, etc. that can be sold as a standard packager and offer a customized package that will allow the customer to request any word that they need to be included in their set. Since these labels weigh next to nothing, shipping can easily be managed with standard mail with usually only a single postage stamp, depending on the delivery address. Make sure you do not claim the next day or two-day delivery for these. Build enough delivery time so you can create and ship the labels without any stress. Once you have an established business model, you can adjust the price and shipping of your product, but more on that later. Check out other Etsy listings to make sure your product pricing is competitive enough, and you are attracting enough potential buyers.

Now, once you have traction in the market, you can offer additional vinyl-based projects like bumper stickers, iron-on, or heat transfer vinyl designs that people can transfer on their clothing using a standard heating iron. Really, once you have gained some clientele, you can modify and customize all your listings to develop into a one-stop-shop for all things of vinyl (a great name for your future Etsy shop, right!).

Selling Finished Pieces

You would be using your Cricut machines for a variety of personal projects like home décor, holiday décor, personalized clothing, and more. Next time you embark on another one of your creative journeys leading to unique creations, just make two of everything, and you can easily put the other product to sell on your Etsy shop. Another great advantage is that you will be able to save all your projects on the Design Space application for future use, so if one of your projects goes viral, you can easily buy the supplies and turn them into money-making offerings. This way, not only your original idea for personal usage will be paid off, but you can make much more money than you invested in it, to begin with.

Again, spend some time researching what kind of designs and decorations are trending in the market and use them to spark up inspiration for your next project. Some of the current market trends include customized cake and cupcake toppers and watercolor designs that can be framed as fancy wall decorations. The cake toppers can be made with cardstock, which is another beginner-friendly material, light in weight, and can be economically shipped tucked inside an envelope.

Personalized Clothing and Accessories

T-shirts with cool designs and phrases are all the rage right now. Just follow a similar approach to the selling vinyl section and take it up a notch. You can create sample clothing with iron-on design and market it with "can be customized further at no extra charge" or "transfer the design on your own clothing" to get traction in the market. You can buy sling bags and customize them with unique designs to be sold as finished products at a higher price than a plain boring sling bag. Consider creating a line of products with a centralized theme like the DC Marvel characters or the Harry Potter movies and design custom t-shirts, hats, and even bodysuits for babies. You can create customized party favor boxes and gift bags at the request of the customer. Once your product has a dedicated customer base, you can get project ideas from them directly and quote them a price for your work. Isn't that great?!?!

Another big advantage of the heat transfer vinyl, as mentioned earlier, is that anyone can transfer the design on their desired item of clothing using a standard household iron. But you would need to include the transfer instructions with the order letting them know exactly how to prep for the heat transfer without damaging their chosen clothing item. And again, heat transfer vinyl can be easily shipped using a standard mailing envelope. We have added a dedicated section on tips for using everyday iron-on with a household iron.

Marketing on Social Media

We are all aware of how social media has become a marketing platform for not only established corporations, but also small businesses and budding entrepreneurs. Simply add hashtags like for sale, product, selling, free shipping, sample included, and more to entice potential buyers. Join Facebook community pages and groups for handcraft sellers and buyers to market your products. Use catchy phrases like customization available at no extra cost or free returns if not satisfied when posting the products on these pages as well as your personal Facebook page. Use Twitter to share feedback from your satisfied customers to widen your customer base. You can do this by creating a satisfaction survey that you can email to your buyers or include a link to your Etsy listing asking for online reviews and ratings from your customers. Another tip here is to post pictures of anything and everything you have created using Cricut machines, even those that you did not plan to sell. You never know who else might need something that you deemed unsellable. Since you will be creating these only after the order has been placed, you can easily gather the required supplies after the fact and get crafting.

Target Local Farmer's Markets and Boutiques

If you like the thrill of a show-and-tell, then reserve a booth at a local farmer's market and show up with some ready-to-sell crafts. In this case, you are relying on the number of people attending and a subset of those who might be interested in making a purchase from you. If you are in an urban neighborhood where people are keenly interested in unique art designs but do not have the time to create them on their own, you can easily make big bucks by setting a decent price point for your products.

Bring flyers to hand out people so they can reach you through one of your social media accounts or email and check all your existing Etsy listings. Think of these events as a means of marketing for those who are not as active online but can be excited with customized products to meet their next big life event like a baby shower, birthday party, or a wedding.

One downside to participating in local events is the generation of mass inventory and booth displays, topped with expenses to load and transport the inventory. You may or may not be able to sell all of the inventory depending on the size of the event, but as I said earlier, you can still make the most of this by marketing your products and building up a local clientele.

And if this information were profitable for you, please leave a review about this book!

The Secrets to Make Money with Your Cricut

In terms of making money from the comfort of your home, you easily achieve that with a Cricut machine. However, you have to bear in mind that there are a number of competitors out there, thus, you have to put in extra effort in order to stand a chance to succeed.

For you to become successful in the Cricut world of crafts, you have to keep the following in mind:

Dare to Be Different

You have to be yourself, unleash your quirkiness and creativity.

Those that have been in the Cricut world of crafts for some time know all about the knockout name tiles. They became a hit and in no time, everyone was producing and selling them. In the crafting world, that is the norm. Thus, you could be among the earliest people to jump on a trend to ride the wave until the next hot seller surfaces. Mind you, that strategy of selling Cricut crafts can become costly and tiresome if you are not careful.

The basic idea here is to add your flair and personal style, and not to completely re-invent the wheel. For example, let's say you come across two name tiles on Etsy, one looks exactly like the other 200+ on sale on the site, while the second one has a few more tweaks and spins on it. The seller of the second product will possibly charge more and accrue a higher profit because his/her product is unique and stands out from the rest.

When you design your products, don't be afraid to tweak your fonts, because even the simplest of tweaks and creativity can make your product stand out from the rest.

Remember this; if you create a product that looks exactly like others, you are only putting yourself in a 'price war,' where no one usually wins.

Keep It Narrow

A lot of crafters out there believe that creating and selling everything under the sun translates into more patronage and more money, but that isn't how it works. On the contrary, it might only result in a huge stock of unsold products, more burn out, and heavy cost. Rather than producing materials here and there, you should focus on being the best in your area of craftiness, so that when people need specific products in your area, they'll come to you.

It can be very tempting to want to spread your tentacles because it might seem like the more you produce, the more options you'll provide for your clients, but that might be counterproductive.

Take out time to think about your area of strength and focus your energy on making products that you'd be known for. It is better to be known as an expert in a particular product than to be renowned for someone that produces a high number of inferior products.

Thus, you should keep it narrow and grow to become the very best in your area of craft.

Be Consistent

If you intend to become successful, you have to work on your Cricut craft business consistently. Some people work once a week or thereabout because they sell as a hobby; however, if you intend to make in-road in your business, you have to work every day.

If you have other engagements and can't work every day, then you should create a weekly schedule and stick to it. If you shun your business for weeks and months at a time, then you will not go anywhere with it.

Apart from consistency in work and production, you also have to be consistent with your product quality and pricing. When your customers are convinced about your products, they will easily recommend you to their friends, family, business partners, and many others.

In business, there are ups and downs, thus, you shouldn't reduce your work rate because things are not going as planned. Success doesn't come easy, but one of the surest ways of being and maintaining success is by consistently doing the things you love.

Be Tenacious

It is not easy to run a business because it involves a lot of hard work, sweat, and even heartbreaks. Thus, you have to bear in mind that there will be days when you will feel like throwing in the towel. There will be days when nothing goes as planned. There will also be days when customers will tick you off. You will feel like a drowning boat because you're working hard but nothing is working out.

However, you have to look at the bigger picture, because the crafting business is not a get-rich-quick scheme. Remember, quitters never win, so quitting isn't an option. Keep doing the things you love, and keep improving. Successful people never give up. They suffer many setbacks but they don't stop.

Thus, for you to be successful in your craft, you have to be tenacious and resilient. Be willing to maneuver your way through tough times, and do not forget to pick up lessons.

Learn Everyday

Be willing to learn from people that have been successful in the business. You don't necessarily have to unravel everything by yourself, because whatever it is you are doing, others have already done it in the past.

Whether you intend to learn how to build a successful Facebook group or how to go up the Etsy ranks, remember that people have already done all that in the past, and are giving out tricks and tips they know.

Make it a tradition to learn something new about your business every day because, at the beginning of your business, you will have to do more marketing than crafting.

When you wake up in the morning, browse through the internet, gather materials, and read in your spare time, because the more you learn, the better your chances of being successful. They say knowledge is power, and for you to become successful as a craftsman/woman, you have to constantly seek new knowledge in the form of tips, tricks, software upgrades, marketing, design ideas, tools, accessories, and many others.

All I am saying is that you should learn without ceasing.

Quality Control

If you intend to grow your brand, you must prioritize the selling of high-quality products. Your motto should quality over everything.

For you to easily succeed, people should know you as someone that sells top-quality products, because quality wins over quantity every day of the week.

You don't want to be known as someone that produces poor quality items because when the word spreads (and it surely will), your business will pack up.

If you focus your attention and efforts on the production of high-quality materials, you will be able to withstand competition, no matter how stiff it is.

Conclusion

Thank you for making it to the end. Now that I have given you several ideas of projects that can be completed with the use of a Cricut, you should have more ideas on how to use your new Cricut machine. Each Cricut is capable of doing some super impressive creative projects.

Keep the tips and tricks provided close by as a reference guide, so you are not searching all over to find the answers to your questions.

Design Space makes Cricut a user-friendly, die-cutter, and I cannot stress enough how much you will get out of the machine as you learn each process. If you are a newbie, start slowly, so you do not become overwhelmed and abandon your machine without giving it a chance.

Frustration is common with first-time users, so read through this book carefully before starting your first project.

Using a Cricut machine should not be a new experience to you by now. However, it would be best if you kept an open mind to new updates. Cricut always give their users a lot of options to choose from, so try as much as possible to carry out extensive research about their products, materials, and subscriptions. Utilizing the tips and tricks in this book is not only going to help you to use your machine for any project that you want, but it will also help you make sure that your machine is in perfect working condition for as long as possible. Many tips and tricks that we have included in this book are things that most people would not have even thought of but are very simple, and they can help your machine last for a lot longer than if you did not try them at all.

If you can utilize the tips in this book, you will be able to keep your machine in great condition and do projects to your heart's content, along with being more skilled. Once you can gain the skills you need, you will be able to go from simple projects to professional projects, and you would be able to see them in a store. These machines are gaining popularity quickly because of all the things that they can work with. It is also a great way to make things for your children or family members and can save you a lot of money in the long run when the holidays come. As such, this machine has even more options and benefits than you thought.

Never stop doing research. Never stop trying new things. Never, ever stop being creative. The Cricut does not make you any less creative; it just makes the process easier so that you can focus your valuable time and efforts on more important things or personalizing the projects after making the cuts. It takes the tedious work out of your hands and makes everything fun, easy, and fast.

One of the greatest things about a Cricut is that it is extremely simple to use. It does take a while to get used to using it, but once you get the hang of it, only your creativity is the limit. With that in mind, this part focuses on giving you a beginner's guide on using the Cricut. Firstly, what comes with your Cricut? That depends on what product you purchase and the money you pay. The more you pay, the more you get.

These don't look like a lot of things, but they are all the right ones to get you started. For a beginner, it is recommended that you purchase a starter set that includes the necessary accessories.

The primary phase in the course of setting up a Cricut is to determine where the machine will be best located. Ideally, the machine will be placed near a computer or tablet, a power source, and where it has room to work. Even if the machine does not require to be hooked to a computer, try to keep it within reach to make the process of loading and unloading easier.

When you purchase your Cricut machine, you will be excited to get started. Search the online Cricut library for ideas on how to create cool projects that will make your environment more enjoyable, as well as projects that you can use to give others joy in their life such as cards and wooden signs.

Now that you have completed this handy manual on how to use the Cricut machine, you should be well-equipped to head out into the Cricut crafting world and start designing your favorite crafts today. Make your first art sale online. In the long run, individuals will be keen on your work and can hardly. Finally, if you would like to feed your newfound Cricut obsession, go right ahead and buy one of the newest Cricut Gypsy. This useful, hand-held apparatus will keep your font cartridges ready for simple portable use. It's possible to design from anyplace on the move, in the physician's office, even while on holiday, or merely sitting on your sofa. Anything you plan on the Gypsy is totally transferable to a Cricut device for die-cutting. If you save your layout, it may be linked to one of your Cricut apparatus and published at a later moment.

I hope you have learned something!

And if you liked the book, why don't you share your opinion with everyone by leaving a nice review?

Thank you so much!

I wish you all the best,

Jennifer Macar

Printed in Great Britain
by Amazon

26531331R00118